MECHANICS' INSTITUTE
☙ MECHANICS' ❧
MERCANTILE LIBRARY

# MECHANICS' INSTITUTE

# Last Rights

*Taking Care with Your Final Journey*

# Last

*Taking Care with
Your Final Journey*

# Rights

## PATRICIA COCHRAN

CAPITAL
BOOKS, INC.
*Sterling, Virginia*

Capital Books, Inc.
P.O. Box 605
Herndon, Virginia 20172-0605

ISBN 1-892123-39-8 (alk. paper)


**Library of Congress Cataloging-in-Publication Data**
Cochran, Patricia Ann.
    Last rights: taking care with your final journey / Patricia Ann Cochran.
    p. cm.
    ISBN 1-892123-39-8
    1. Death--Handbooks, manuals, etc. 2. Funeral rites and ceremonies--Handbooks, manuals, etc. I. Title.

GT3150.C575 2000
393--dc21                                                                00-056456


Printed in Canada on acid-free paper that meets the American National Standards Institute Z39-48 Standard.

First Edition

10 9 8 7 6 5 4 3 2 1

# to my readers

Death is not a topic, but a reality—we fear it, we deny it, we embrace it, and always we grieve it. But to write about it is to make it topical. So I ask that you forgive the places where it might seem as such and look through the words to the places that touch that reality for you.

with a grateful heart
to
Dennis and Teresa
whose gift of time allowed this book to be written

In memory of
Julia Mayo
1942 – 1991
whose spirit guided mine

# contents

# prologue

*P*aul died suddenly . . . in the early morning on a tennis court, doing what he loved to do. We were to have dinner with Carol and him that evening. Instead we spent the morning with her as the shock of his death slowly penetrated the layers of her being, traveling insidiously until a few hours into the reality it left her dazed and confused.

And still so many things to consider: What funeral home to call? Having just recently joined a synagogue and not really known by that community, whom to contact? What would Paul want in the way of a service? How would he want to be remembered?

Questions abounded with no clear answers as Carol fought to maintain her focus. There was no plan for this, no prearrangement save for a family burial space in another state, no faith community to draw on—just snatches and pieces of information that we attempted to knit together while in a state of disbelief.

It drove home for me, and for those few gathered with Carol, the urgent need to plan for this random time when death comes. We thought it, even as we ministered to her, each of us feeling the threat of loss by association. And then one person, Paul's cousin the doctor, spoke.

"I haven't done anything to prepare," he said, as his thoughts raced ahead to their own finish line. And then, almost as if to himself, "I guess we can never really prepare."

We can never really prepare for a sudden loss, I agree, but we can start to plan—for our own leaving—so that at the end stages of life, we and our loved ones can be held, and listened to, and ministered to, and rest, instead of being peppered with questions, and forced to oversee a series of transactions that rob all of us of the tender period that marks the last stage of life, and—if we are suddenly gone from them—the tender period that marks the beginning of life without us.

We all will die. This is your opportunity to start to plan.

# introduction

Who am I to speak to you about death? I am you. I am not a credentialed spokesperson who has spent many years developing a body of work. At first that disturbed me. And then I remembered that as a mere mortal, I am eminently qualified, as are you, to speak of death, because, like you, death has brushed up against me. It claimed people on my periphery and close friends before moving into my family. More recently, it claimed my father. In the in-between, I wrote this book.

Writing this book came as a "call," which I define as "an irresistible, unwavering impulse to do a thing," even a hard thing. This "thing" I initially questioned. Shouldn't I be studying this topic before presuming to write a book about it? Will you listen to a mere mortal? Each time the answer came in a stillness, and the words were these: You have had your life experiences to draw from; you have been with the dying; you have attended to the survivors; you have planned a service for the terminally ill and for those who have died; you have been present in the aftermath of two suicides; you have helped others to write eulogies for their loved ones and delivered eulogies for loved ones; and you have helped many with their disposition arrangements. You know everything you need to know by virtue of these experiences, and recorded in your cells as a mortal being is the landscape of death if you would only let it be divulged to you.

I learned to trust that voice, to say yes, and then to start writing. As I wrote I was aware that what materialized in the form of this book did not come from me but through me. I read very little of what was already written about death and dying until after the manuscript was finished. It was then that I realized that my thoughts fit into the universal whole—they dovetailed with the writings of others—which then set me to wondering: How did I know these things? And are these new concepts worthy of a book?

My answer to myself and from the professionals in the field of death and dying who have reviewed the manuscript and supported this effort is yes! And from the many big-hearted people who shared their stories of loss and grief with me, another yes! Yes, because each of us becomes a unique filter of a universal truth, and when we get out of our own way and let it come, it resonates as true with those who hear it.

I am you, a mere mortal, having a unique human experience, and it is from this perspective that I share these words with you. They are yours and mine commingled and emerging from our common humanity and our common fear of the unknown. But is death an unknown? Celtic poet John O'Donohue, author of *Eternal Echoes*, offers this:

> When you were born, there was a presence that came
> into the world with you. The reason no one noticed it
> is because everyone was so excited about greeting *you!*
> It is your secret companion; it has walked with you
> and has kept step with you throughout your lifetime.
> It is with you now and will remain with you until you
> leave this earth. That presence is the Light of Death.

It is this "Light of Death" that I now ask you to consider, to acknowledge, and to invite in, as you read through these pages. If they prove helpful, as I believe they will, it will be my privilege to have served you.

This book is meant for you, of all ages, all religions, in all conditions of life, because all of us are mortal human beings. We are born and we will die. If we are breathing today, inevitably there will come a day when we will stop breathing. In your breathing days, I encourage you to look to the unforeseeable future by planning thoughtfully and lovingly for your death and for the disposition of your physical body. This book is designed to help you with that process. You may also use it to broach the subject of death with parents, children, aged relatives, or people with a life-ending condition.

Our generation will have many experiences with death as we continue to age together. Although many of us are aware of the necessary realities that accompany death, few of us act on them.

This guide is designed to inspire you to want to do a hard thing— plan for your death—which then enables you to help others do likewise, and strengthens you to help those whose time is now. Outlined here for you are the issues of importance that surround death, along with the forms you will need to finalize those issues. Personal stories, poems, and quotations move you along, for it is often through other people's stories that the most useful information is gleaned.

This is an opportunity for us in this never-say-die culture to model for each other and for our children how to face death. There is no right or wrong way. It will be as individual as our own births, our own lives, and our relationships with each other. Death does not demand uniformity. We will each come in our own way informed by whatever shapes and anchors our lives.

Resistance, fear, and anxiety are part of the equation as we cross the paradoxical bridge of wanting life while accepting death. You will have your own thoughts to share with each other. Some you have already shared with me. We have talked about it in parking lots, at the beach, watching a tennis match, at dinner parties, and in small groups. Sometimes you have invited more information with your comments, and sometimes you have used them to stop me cold.

These have been some of our conversations . . .

> "I cannot talk about death with my husband or my children. I couldn't bear the thought of them missing me, not having me here."

How can we hope to have them bear that loss if we do not talk about the possibility of our dying? Talk about it at the dinner table, with family, with friends, with each other, so that dying becomes a part of living.

> "I'm uncomfortable around someone who is dying and don't know what to say. It is so sad!"

Think of how sad and lonely the dying person must be to have no one to talk with.

"Death scares me."

Many of us, as baby boomers, learned in natural childbirth classes, with husbands and loved ones coaching us, how to bring children into the world—a traumatic trip for them, from the safety of the womb, to a long arduous journey through the canal, from a watery existence to the first violent intake of air, the first breath that carried the pink flush of oxygen and life the length of their tiny purple forms. We bridged that fear of not knowing by practicing conscious and intentional ways of helping the process.

Death is simply the reverse. We struggle with the process of giving up what at first we never needed—precious air—to revert to our watery state.

It is this struggle, I believe, that scares us—not death itself, but dying a slow death. With more of the medical community becoming educated in the art of being with and caring for the dying, palliative approaches promise us a death where physically, emotionally, spiritually, and mentally we are not abandoned to the dying process, but nurtured until our very last breath. That is our wish and one that can be achieved if we engage in a collaborative partnership and together defy the taboo of talking about death.

Some of us pray for a quick end. Others pray for a time of introduction—to get used to the reality of dying, to take care of unfinished business. Since we do not know when death will come, this book will help us to prepare for the unknowable. It is organized in journal fashion so that you will make it your own and add and delete as you wish. All of the forms used are contained in the back section. Legal forms are included as sample documents. Use these as a model to gather all the information you will need to complete these documents, and then seek legal counsel to finalize them. You will not need a lawyer to complete a Living Will or to choose your Healthcare Proxy.

Many of these forms represent the tangible areas outside of ourselves, the acquisitions of a lifetime. The intangibles are revealed in documents like the Living Will (which takes effect while you are still alive) and in personal stories. And since planning and preparing for death is more than filling out forms, I encourage you to read through to the end. A thought expressed here might provoke another in you that you might wish to write down and share with your family.

As with birthing, let us learn at the end time of life how to help each other transition once again. Let us model for each other the experience of dying and teach our children, whom we brought forth, how to send us forth. Let us share this information freely with each other—the powerful secret that we are, all of us, going to die—one hundred percent of us for sure! And let us complete the responsibility of parenting with this final lesson—that death is an integral part of the process of living.

In his instructive book, *The Seven Habits of Highly Effective People*, Steven Covey obliges us to "Begin with the End in Mind." I hope this book will instill this habit in you and pull you gently into completing your final arrangements so that, having planned for your leaving, and having talked about it freely with each other, you might turn more fully into life and living. These are your last rights. Address them with great care.

> To give light to them that sit in darkness
> and in the shadow of death,
> to guide our feet into the way of peace.
>> Luke 1:79
>> (KJV)

# Frankie's Story

In our Western Anglo culture, life is full of strife. From the cradle to the grave, we are continually striving—striving for approval, striving to get ahead, striving to be the best at whatever, striving to beat the odds.

Through the study and practice of Taoist and C'han (Zen) philosophy, I came to understand that life on earth is simply a natural process that one goes through, and is not, as I had been taught to believe, some sort of unequal cosmic contest. I learned among other things, that trying softer is preferable to trying harder, and, paradoxically, that change is the one constant. Absolutely beyond one's power, change is inevitable and irresistible. One can choose fruitlessly to stem the tide and/or to rail in vain against it; or instead choose to accept and embrace it, observing with wonder its processes at every level of existence. I have chosen the latter course in my later life.

Once freed of the exhausting burden of continuous striving, I have come to find nearly every aspect of life itself to be interesting, to be observed, savored, and enjoyed. At the same time, the clichéd metaphors of life and death struggles have lost all their meaning for me.

> *Francis "Frankie" Marco Leonard, Jr.*
> *(Fen Chi to his Chinese friends), 52,*
> *departed this life to begin his next*
> *adventure in another realm.*

# living your eulogy

Each year I celebrate the anniversary of the
day I was diagnosed with cancer because
that terrible day began my transformation
into the person I wanted to become . . .

Dennis Cochran
year 5 after cancer

*I*f you begin with the end in mind, a good place to start is to write your
eulogy today. Wondrous things can happen with this exercise. You can
review your yesterdays and preview your tomorrows. By that I mean that
if the person being revealed as you write is not to your liking, you still
have the time to become the person you would enjoy writing about—a
preview of things to come! And in reviewing your life, you begin to credit
yourself for all of your accomplishments. You begin to affirm your gifts
and track the continuum of your growth and development.

A eulogy speaks to the essence of you, what defines you as the
unique individual you are. It speaks to your character, your attributes,
and to how you approach life. The word *eulogy* means "good words."
Traditionally written by others, a eulogy is meant to extol and praise.
But because you are writing your own eulogy and because the image
you hold is not yet distorted by loss, you might achieve more balance
and might reveal a more authentic rendering. Who else knows you at
this most intimate level? And at this most intimate level the long and
short of our life's stories are revealed.

Your eulogy should be evolutionary . . . to be continued . . . the
person you are today as you write may not be the same person you are
tomorrow. To do a life review now in this way is to identify, internalize,
and develop the character traits that will serve you in the rest of your
tomorrows.

When others eulogize us, they address what we have been to them. But only we can address who we are to ourselves as we stand in service to others. Try it! You won't believe the excitement it stirs in you! Here is a chance to touch your passionate self. Remember, paint yourself in color! Your obituary will contain the facts of your life, the black and white you, and announce the day of your death. Your eulogy, however, will contain the essence of you and will define your life for all time, and in living color! Turn to page 11 and begin . . .

# Sample Eulogy

I loved to dance. It freed me up like nothing else. I loved beautiful things—to make art, to wear art, to gaze on art, and to see the beauty in the whole as well as in the brokenness. I loved to decorate, to design, to create a reflection of a person's uniqueness in the physical environment. I was giving, sometimes to the detriment of myself, and learning to maintain a balance had not been easy.

I was intolerant of injustice. I did not believe in disposable people. I was impatient, a risk taker, noisy and angry, yet always I sought and found ways to regain a sense of peace and harmony. I was a fierce mother and protector of my children, and in social settings, would play the devil's advocate as a spontaneous and potentially combustible backboard. I was stimulating and stimulated and always passionate.

If you knew me, you knew that I was an experiential learner. I learned by doing. I pricked and probed brains and hearts and souls. I liked to tell my stories and I listened to yours. I thought we should all have told our stories to each other. That is how I believed we learn. So I would like to leave you with three stories that have helped to shape my being.

The first came from Charlie—I was just starting my business, Pioneer Custom Cleaning, a home and office cleaning service, and was not sure how my family and friends would respond. I believed they would feel ashamed and embarrassed. They were initially, but Charlie said, "Hold your head up, and remember, it's not the job that dignifies the person, but the person who dignifies the job." Fifteen years later, I was still serving in Pioneer Custom Cleaning as part of a team and family of professional cleaners. I had come to believe that many of our country's ills would have been solved or at least put into perspective if each one of us was made to clean another's toilet at least once a month.

The second story came from my friend, Diane—I had been in a faith community for a few years, always wandering the periphery as an observer, never risking being known, and feeling very lonely. Diane took hold of me and said, "You know why we don't trust you? You won't show us who you are!" And she was right. I worked to present a perfect façade. If a crack appeared in the façade, I would hurry out to brick and mortar it before returning my seemingly perfect self to the group. It was exhausting! Diane's gift provoked me to show the cracks, to be vulnerable, to trust others and risk intimacy. I took baby steps at first, then, as the toxins seeped out of the cracks that I dared to let show, the love poured in; and—my fear went away. I came to believe that fear and love cannot co-exist. One will always yield to the other. I chose love.

My third story came by way of Ruth, who was in the middle stage of Alzheimer's disease—I sometimes drove her to and from church and took her on walks. She would budge, or not. I never knew when either would happen—to get her in or out of the car, to get her to rise or be seated, or to stop or go. This particular day, we were walking. I was an always-in-motion kind of woman, and Ruth became transfixed by a bed of flowers. I was intent on moving her along, but she would not budge. So I was forced to stand and wait with her. After a long while, in the face of my impatience, she said softly, "Have you ever seen such a blue?" And I had never, until I saw through her eyes. I remembered that always, when I was in a hurry, when I was in nature, or interacting with people, or moving into an unknown. I would think, "Have you ever seen such a blue?" And then my eyes would open wide so as not to miss it.

These are my stories and my gift to you. They reminded me to serve others, let the warmth in, and keep a wide-eyed wonder about life so that, "Have you ever seen such a blue?" will echo in all that you are and do.

I was blessed to be here, to love and be loved by you, and blessed again to be journeying home. Remember me always because I will be forever loving you . . .

*And the point is*
*To live everything*
*Live the questions now*
*perhaps you will then gradually*
*without noticing it*
*Live along some distant day*
*into the answer.*

Rainer Maria Rilke
(1875–1926)

# My Eulogy

# your obituary

You've written about what makes you unique. Now you need to list your vital statistics, your survivors, and the achievements and recognitions that have given meaning to your life. This factual information will then become the framework of your obituary, and can be enhanced by borrowing interesting information and insights from your self-written eulogy.

Check with your local newspapers on their approach to obituaries. These are usually published free of charge and at the discretion of the editors. In a major publication, where space is limited, usually a connection to the community is warranted to receive an obituary. Expect some editing. Also, since there is a two- to three-day delay before publication, it is important to notify the paper as soon as the death occurs. Your family is usually responsible for placing an obituary. This is not to be confused with a *death notice* that is usually supplied to the appropriate outlets by your funeral director. Expect a charge for a death notice. Some papers will run a picture of the deceased with the notice, and others will not.

Whether or not your obituary appears in a public medium, it is an important biographical snapshot that can be used in the memorial program (see Chapter 10) and distributed at a service of remembrance.

# Key Information for Your Obituary

Name: _____
First                          Middle                          Last

Maiden Name: _____

Street Address: _____

City: _____ State: _____ Zip: _____

Date of Birth: _____ Place of Birth: _____

Organization (or retired from): _____

Employer: _____ Years: _____

Marital Status: _____

Children: _____

Grandchildren: _____

Educational Institutions Attended: _____

_____

Degrees Received: _____

_____

Fraternities/Honor Societies: _____

_____

Military/Years/Rank: 

Civic or Public Offices Held: 

Special Achievements and Recognitions: 

Hobbies/Special Interests: 

Contact Person: 

Telephone Number to Verify Information:

# My Survivors

Be sure to list the city and state where each person lives.

Spouse/Partner: _____

_____

Former Spouses: _____

_____

Children: _____

_____

Stepchildren: _____

_____

Grandchildren: _____

_____

Parents: _____

_____

Stepparents: _____

_____

Grandparents: _____

_____

Brothers: _____

_____

Sisters: _____

_____

Others: _____

_____

Preceded in death by: _____

_____

Pets: _____

_____

# My Obituary

You now have a general outline for your obituary. Now start to write, remembering to include other interesting information from your eulogy. Both your eulogy and your obituary should be updated periodically as you continue to stretch and grow in the years ahead. They also become an important source of information for others designated to eulogize you, and especially so in a religious service when you might not be known to the officiant.

You can also include a picture with your obituary and sometimes with a death notice. There often is no standard size, but the photograph should be clear. Place your choice of picture below:

In our transient and small-world society, you may have moved around a bit. You might want to have your obituary and/or death notice printed in the papers of those locales.

I would like my obituary and/or death notice to appear in the following newspapers and/or publications:

_____

_____

_____

_____

❧

> *Not only is there but one way of doing things rightly,*
> *but there is only one way of seeing them, and that is,*
> *seeing the whole of them.*

John Ruskin
(1884–1946)

# Dennis's Story

It's been over five years now. Mother died first. She was a teacher of grammar, of homework, of politeness, of swimming. She seemed to move into death so quickly. I guess I never really expected that she would die. There was no time to pull anything together with her, to have any fun, to try to find out all the stuff I didn't know about her so I could feel a little closer to her. She was an orphan and had no models for how to hold people. I remember, as an adult, I took her arms one day and demonstrated by bringing them around me how I needed to be held. That was a breakthrough.

She died of emphysema. When I was a teenager she would come up to my room and we would hang together blowing our cigarette smoke out the window so Dad would not suspect. Those times were great. Three days before she died I fed her like a child, making airplane noises as I maneuvered the spoonfuls of applesauce into her mouth and down a searing throat filled with thrush from her medication. All the signs were there, I just chose to avoid them. And then there was no more time.

Dad became closer to me after Mom died. We were becoming intimate, and I felt for the first time a genuine love and affection from him. We were becoming pals. I always knew cognitively that he would be there for me in times of crisis and would support me always, but I never had a sense that he wanted to be with me on my own turf. We played tennis together, shot pool together. Dad was a singer and a performer, and I started singing lessons.

He pined for Mom. They were together for fifty-three years. Sometimes while visiting us, when the missing got too intense, he would crawl in bed with my wife and me and snuggle between us to experience being held again. But the cancer re-emerged, and within two years of Mom's death, he was gone.

My biggest regret with Mom is that I allowed her to pass the phone to Dad quickly, because she always assumed that he was the reason I had called. Now, with both of them gone, I cannot call either and really still want to connect. The feeling is similar to calling someone, the phone ringing beyond patience, and, frustratingly, there isn't even an answering machine. No one picks up. You look back and try to fill in the blanks with your own children, even grown children, as you try to repair any damage they might have sustained from your own parenting, because you don't want them to feel this void when you're gone. They're gone now, and the cycle swings back to you. It's hard and, yet, strangely freeing.

## Connections

In the fall of my years
I feel spiraling
Winter and wonder
how warm/cold/friendly
or anti will Death be—
Will it cradle me
or rock me hard?
Either way—expanding
I look forward to my ABCs
in the seminar on afterlife
preparing me (for or if) I return
Until that happens, know this:
I deplore pain
Pray for serenity
Will continue on to the very last exit
to struggle for Peace/Equality/Freedom
I shall not go quietly
But shout my last haloo.

Phil Sosis

# introduction to estate planning

*3*

$I$f you choose not to go quietly then you must have a plan, a whole range of plans. In other words, you must do some estate planning. This is not just for the wealthy. This "estate" is your "condition of being," and it includes a Durable Power of Attorney, your Last Will and Testament, your Living Will, and a Durable Power of Attorney for Healthcare.

What are these documents? Can you leave this world without them? Yes, but not comfortably. These legal documents are like some medicines, hard to digest, but good for you. If you don't have them, the cleanup for those who survive you is quite messy. Let's look at them.

First, if you are out of commission temporarily or permanently, either physically or emotionally, your Durable Power of Attorney will cover you until you are back in action and even after you die. Why? Because this document shows that you have chosen someone to act and speak on your behalf in both legal and financial matters. In other words, it empowers someone to manage your affairs when you are unable to do so.

Second, your Last Will and Testament ensures that the things you have spent a lifetime collecting go to the people you choose (your beneficiaries). It also names the person you want to be in charge of making sure that happens (the executor), and it can name a guardian for your minor children. In addition, because you like the last word, your will can also include a "Statement of Wishes." This last one, of course, is not legally binding, but probably the most fun to compile. It includes such things as: I want Billy to continue to develop his talent for cartooning and *do something with it*; and I want my girls to forgive themselves more and know that *they don't have to be perfect*; and, I want my husband to relax his lips and *practice smiling* more often. Things like that!

Third, a Living Will allows you to choose what kinds of medical intervention you want if you are terminally ill or in a persistent vegetative state. With advances in medical technology, we now have the means to prolong life long after death becomes an inevitability. This important document protects your choices.

Fourth, if you have completed your living will and you want to further strengthen it, you will need a Durable Power of Attorney for Healthcare, which means that you have named a spokesperson and given that person authority to make sure that your wishes are heard should you suffer a medical crisis. These last two are commonly known as Advance Medical Directives.

There it is! All of the above four documents are designed to give you a voice in your own affairs, even after death. They give your loved ones the authority they need to act on your behalf, and relieve their burden of making major decisions without the benefit of knowing your wishes.

In the Appendix are guides to each of these important tools and sample forms waiting for your input. These forms are designed to acquaint you with the process and to guide you through the procedures. The forms are a beginning and are meant to spark planning for your leaving. As with all legal documents, you should seek legal advice and counsel tailored to your individual circumstances, remembering that . . .

Even if death were to fall upon you today
like lightning, you must be ready to die
without sadness and regret, without any
residue of clinging for what is left behind.
Remaining in the recognition of the absolute
view, you should leave this life like an eagle
soaring up into the blue sky.

Dilgo Khyentse Rinpoche

# Patsy's Story

It wasn't that we didn't know Dad was dying. It was that
we wanted him to know. We wanted, all of us, to be freed
from the pretense of "not knowing" so that we could say
the things we needed to say to him. So we asked
the doctor for answers that never came.

He had been Dad's physician for a long time,
someone Dad trusted. And whether it was his inability to speak of
death or his perception that Dad did not want to know remains a
mystery. But this doctor could not say the words. When we pressed, he
would actually wink at us between noncommittal and vague phrases as
if to say, "You're all bright. Figure out what I'm not saying."

Talking to Dad about death then was next to impossible. He would
not let us in. I asked him once if he was afraid of dying. He responded
tersely that he didn't know enough about it to be afraid. Dad had a way
of answering that warned you off any further discussion of a subject he
chose not to address.

I remember when we gathered at the table for what we all knew
would be his last Thanksgiving with us and prayed for grace for him on
the road ahead. At his turn, Dad shot back, "I can see you've all written
me off but I pray that God will grant me a miracle and rid me of this
cancer." He was angry and seemed to be blaming us for what his doctor
could not say.

We were helpless then and painfully stuffed, with unsaid words, unshed tears, and with the certainty that time was running out for all of us. It would have helped if the person he trusted with his life, his doctor, could have helped him with his dying.

I don't know . . . maybe it would have eased our pain, his and ours.

Let's all agree on this and call it . . .

# the patient's creed

1. To teach our doctors about dying.
2. To instruct them to know the limits of medical care.
3. To forgive them for not knowing.
4. To invite them to our deathbed to share the journey.
5. To encourage them to keep on caring by saying the words, "I'm sorry. We've done all we can. How can we help you now to die?"

> All these years later, I accept what the ancients knew: All [people] must die and death is not to be feared. There is a Light that we will all experience after death, and that Light represents joy, peace, and unconditional love.
>
> Melvin Morse, M.D. with Paul Berry
> *Closer to the Light*
> (*Learning from the Near-Death*
> *Experiences of Children*)
> Melvin Morse M.D.

---

Note: Training programs have been developed in certain states to teach medical students how to work with terminally ill patients. These programs are designed to fill in the gap between the limits of medical science and death. Along with classroom curricula on pain management and comfort care, students make home visits to the terminally ill in the company of hospice nurses. These supervised field trips bring home to young medical students the fullness of the dying experience.

# advance
## medical directives

And now we start to plan . . . because,
If you do not change directions, you
end up where you are heading.

Old Chinese Proverb

A dvance Medical Directives is an umbrella term. Think of it as a "Quality Life Assurance Plan." Whatever you have determined defines a quality life for you is described in your Advance Medical Directives or the instructions you wish to have followed in case of a medical crisis. These directives include a Living Will and a Durable Power of Attorney for Healthcare.

The use of Advance Directives is your right according to federal legislation known as The Patient's Self Determination Act of 1991. This law states that all healthcare institutions participating in Medicaid or Medicare are required to advise you about your right to participate in medical decision making, including the right to refuse treatment under applicable state laws.

Writing an Advance Directive is your insurance against the use of medical technology to sustain your body beyond the scope of life and living as you define it. Using it can prevent exploitation of the aged and the incapacitated, keep some situations out of courts, and influence medical costs for families.

Advance Directives introduce choices into the medical equation. Coupled with involving your active community, they represent your greatest asset for freedom of choice. Therefore, in addition to written directives, you need to discuss your wishes with the people closest to you—with your family; your friends; your doctors; spiritual leaders; and, especially, with your healthcare spokesperson.

The next few pages talk about the two components that make up an Advance Directive. First, the Living Will. But first, a thought . . .

In the beginning
we learned from each other
     how to die,
before
the naturalness of death
     was taken from us,
replaced with a technological wedge
     corrupting nature's way,
denying to ourselves and to each other
     that death will come.
Yielding then to the inevitable,
     we shatter into pieces of shock
        and grief
     that require an industry
        of professionals
          to put us back
            together
            again,
     and to teach us
        to accept
          that which we already know
     from the beginning.

*The fact that you are not dead is not*
*sufficient proof that you are alive . . .*

Brother David Steindl-Rast
*Gratefulness, The Heart of Prayer*

# Introduction to the Living Will

Some things we take for granted: breath, the ability to eat and drink, to think. When we consider what our lives would be like without certain faculties, how many of us would name these? What are the parameters that define a quality life for us? What does it mean to be in a persistent vegetative state?

These are the hard issues that a Living Will addresses. Everyone should have one, not only for your own protection, but to protect your families by removing the burden of deciding for another what is a quality life, a viable life.

In legal and clinical terms, a Living Will can seem formidable and even frightening, but in the terms of our everyday life, of the essence that defines us, in our own words, it might seem less so.

Start now to write your definition of a precious life, and share it with your family, your friends, your doctors, your spiritual leaders, and your healthcare spokesperson. In addition to accepting or rejecting specific treatment choices, such as artificial feeding and forced breathing with a respirator, talk about your values and what life means to you. Having a sense of the values you hold will help your family when you are facing a medical crisis.

We have all heard and read about the families who have been tortured by these kinds of decisions. Their experiences speak volumes, the lesson being that we must choose for ourselves not only what gives our life meaning, but also what gives our death meaning, and make both active and rich. The future benefit is to our families; the immediate benefit is to us in that to list these abilities is to take these precious gifts for granted no longer.

# Helpful Information
# for Writing My Living Will

The Living Will evolved from people writing letters to each other and to their doctors about their wishes for their own medical treatment should they be rendered unable to voice them. Today, that concept is enhanced further by naming a spokesperson or healthcare proxy to carry out those wishes.

Basically, the Living Will document allows you to make decisions regarding life-sustaining procedures if you are in a persistent vegetative state. Life-sustaining procedures may include mechanical ventilation and/or artificial nutrition and hydration (eating and drinking), withholding CPR, antibiotics, or kidney dialysis.

Persons in a *persistent vegetative state* still have an intact brain stem that can regulate vital body functions, so they can survive for many years even though they are unable to respond to their environment.

*Please know that decisions to withhold or withdraw life-sustaining procedures in no way affect procedures used for comfort and pain management.*

There is strong evidence that death by dehydration may be the easiest, most gentle death for many patients as long as the dying patient's lips remain moistened.

For terminally ill patients, some benefits of dehydration include less fluid in the lungs and less congestion; less fluid in the throat requiring less suctioning; and less pressure around tumors resulting in less pain.

There is also clinical evidence that both advanced age and neurological damage can diminish a person's sense of thirst and that, under these conditions, the body may produce its own pain-killing substances.

*You do not need legal counsel to complete a Living Will. It should be signed and witnessed by two people, and copies given to your family, your doctor, and your healthcare spokesperson(s).*

---

Note: Eighty percent of all deaths in the United States are accompanied with an intentional decision to withhold or withdraw treatment. Source: *Hard Choices for Loving People* by Hank Dunn.

> *No passion so effectually robs the mind of all its powers of acting and*
> *reasoning as fear.*
>
> Edmund Burke
> (1729–1797)

# Dad's Story

On Tuesday the phone rang. It was Hennie, a longtime companion of Dad's calling from Florida. Dad was in the hospital hooked up to life support. There must be some mistake, I countered. He had beaten lung cancer. How could he now suddenly be dying? He had just celebrated his eighty-fifth birthday a few weeks earlier. Having ascertained that he was stable, I alerted the family scattered on the east and west coasts and drove the seventeen hours from Maryland directly to the hospital in Miami Beach. When I arrived, they were preparing to move Dad downstairs for a CT scan. There was just time for an embrace to tell him I was there, and then he was wheeled out. It was late in the evening, and no doctor was available to talk with me. I was advised by the nurse that the situation was critical, so I spent the rest of the evening calling family, preparing them, as each one made arrangements to fly in. Hennie and I then went back to Dad's apartment and talked late into the night.

He had not been feeling well, she thought, for a few weeks. He seemed agitated and restless and his breathing was shallow. Finally, she bullied him into going to the hospital on the Friday before I arrived. It was now the following Thursday. At the hospital, he was diagnosed with pneumonia and admitted. But Dad's terror of hospitals and his fear of dying overcame him, and none of his doctor's pleas to remain and be treated could dissuade him from signing himself out and returning home. He spent a restless weekend and by Monday was unable to walk from the bedroom to the living room. He had also begun to shake violently, and Hennie again forced him back to the hospital where later that evening he suffered respiratory and cardiac arrest.

The day following my arrival I spoke with the doctor who had worked on Dad immediately after his heart stopped. He said they were unable to get a pulse for fifteen minutes before they finally brought him back to life. His brain was without oxygen for fifteen minutes! I knew after seeing Dad again that morning that he was no longer with us. Dad was gone, erased from his body by a lack of oxygen to his brain, and this doctor was confirming my worse fears. Why, I asked, knowing he would be severely brain damaged, would you put him on life support? Why didn't you just let him die? The horror of all that I had learned in writing this guide was flashing before me. We did not have a do not resuscitate (DNR) order, he responded. We were obliged to continue our efforts to bring him back.

Dad did not have a living will. During my three-week stay with him the previous summer before and after the lung surgery, he had refused to talk about it. During the admittance procedure to this well-known hospital in Miami Beach, I was shocked to find out that no one had spoken with him about a living will. I finally asked, and they seemed bewildered as they searched for the form. In response to their request, however, he did name me as his healthcare spokesperson. Even as he gave my name to the admitting nurse, I knew he had no under-standing of what that meant. With a wave of his hand in irritation, he wanted the subject dismissed. But I had him sign the form, found two witnesses, and had it notarized. I remembered to bring this document with me now and had it put into his file.

This doctor was telling me that they look for signs of recovery in a patient at least twelve hours after this kind of collapse, and Dad was still not responding after forty-eight hours. The signs were not good. A ventilator was doing the majority of his breathing; antibiotics for the pneumonia and food and water were all being given to him intra-venously. And Dad was not in his body to receive any of it. I was glad for a merciful God who stole him away before the assault. He would not have been able to bear it.

I talked then to this doctor about removing the life support, and he agreed that was a reasonable request. I also said that, given the situation, I wanted my brothers and sister to be present also and that even though I had the power to act as his healthcare proxy, I wanted it to be a shared decision among his children.

By Friday afternoon, the fourth day with no response from Dad, the family started to trickle in. I went back and forth to the airport for their staggered arrivals. In the meantime an EEG was done that showed minimal brain activity, and Hennie was now able to admit that there was no hope of recovery. She had been stirred to hopefulness when Dad's eyelids would drift open even as his pupils rolled out of sight. And she had interpreted his occasional involuntary yawns as a sign of recovery. The doctors' remarks to me and the occasional comments of the nurses about reflexive movements had convinced her otherwise. Hennie's acceptance helped to support me emotionally for the difficult task ahead.

My older brother shared Dad's aversion to sickness and hospitals; my younger brother was a silent, observing presence; and my sister, eleven years younger than I, had not experienced death. We had convinced my mother, long divorced from my father, to come and be with us and, all told, with the grown grandchildren and the spouses we numbered ten. And not one among the ten of us could claim a close relationship with Dad. He was, by choice, a fringe member of the family, but here we all were now, gathering for him and for us—reconciling for our own selves who he was to us and for us, and knowing instinctively that to do otherwise would render us stuck. I was so proud of who we are and so in love with all of them and with my Dad.

For me, it had been a long journey from last summer to this day. Last year I had driven back from Florida to my home in Maryland, alone with my thoughts and my anguish after a difficult three weeks of being with him during his surgery. Before the diagnosis of lung cancer and the subsequent surgery, Dad had never been seriously ill and had never required a hospital stay. He was angry at his body's betrayal and scared almost to paralysis of the consequences, which he had convinced himself were dire. His body shook with fear as we traversed the parking lot on his way to be admitted. He fought all of us—the doctors, the nurses, his other companion, and especially me. He cursed his condition and all of us. His body was so weakened with the fight and the surgery that he could not sit upright a week after the surgery, and still he fought to leave the hospital. His doctor, two social workers, and a psychiatrist all pleaded with him to no avail to remain for rehab and regain his strength. My only recourse then was to admit defeat, to tell him I loved him, and to let him know that if he chose to go against his doctor's

orders I would be leaving in my car in the next instant to return home
to my family. It worked!

A few days into rehab he was convinced that it was the right
decision, and he thanked me and misted over as I left to drive back
home to Maryland. Hennie would arrive to nurse him on his return
from the hospital's rehab unit.

The ride home, however, tripped a switch in my head that played
back the pictures of my father and me. I watched it through the sun and
the clouds and the rain and the tears of the long journey home. The first
day I watched. The second day I recorded, sometimes sobbing through
the words, rendering them incomprehensible in places. When I arrived
home, I spent long hours transcribing all of my tears and anguish and
hurt and missed connections with my father. Every cell that held a
memory I emptied until there was nothing left to recover. I read our life
story over and over until I began to understand my father and where he
came from, and to understand the lack in him that caused the incom-
pleteness in me. Then I gave copies to my brother and sister, to my
minister, and to a few trusted friends. I wanted it all exposed. And then
I forgave him. Just a few weeks before the call telling me he was hooked
up to life support, I had gone into the computer and erased all traces of
that accounting and had torn up the hard copies of our past. My
forgiveness was complete, so that when I arrived in Florida and saw my
father lying there hooked up to artificial life, I was filled with love for
him, and knew deep in my soul that this was no longer what he wanted.

It was Friday night, and all but two of us had arrived. I first took
my brothers and sister in to see him. "Wake up Daddy," my sister said,
"It's me, Gerri, wake up." Then my younger brother, Butch said, "Didn't
anyone tell the doctors that's how Dad always slept. He's just sleeping!"
My older brother, Ashley, watched saying little, and I watched him as a
knowing gradually took hold and I knew he was already understanding.

The grandchildren went in by twos and threes and I told each of
them what I had learned from the doctors. My sister wanted to hear it
all firsthand and she opted to spend the night at his bedside. We all
agreed that she needed this time with him to move into acceptance. In
her wish to help, Hennie tried to push everyone there prematurely, and
I gently reminded her that it had taken her days to accept what we were
asking them to do in an hour. We all left my sister to her vigil.

When I arrived the next day, Saturday, she was filled with news about how the doctor had advised her to wait another five days at least, and how, she said, they agreed that I was rushing the process. I disagreed. She said I was trying to kill our father. I said he needed us to be strong, that if we waited for the antibiotics to treat the pneumonia, we would have no way to help Dad leave, that he at least deserved a chance for his own breath to sustain him. She needed to talk with one more doctor, and then I knew she couldn't move there and knew the doctors, understanding her reluctance, were supporting her resistance. I felt angry and helpless and told her I would fight for his right to die with some measure of dignity. I walked out with my daughters comforting me. We sat, all of us, outside the hospital while I cried and railed against the doctors, my sister, our family's penchant to communicate with jokes, my father's vanity, and him lying there helpless with his tongue hanging out and everyone watching, watching, watching. I was glad he wasn't in his body to witness it.

"No more joking," I said. I wanted it over and I cried uncontrollably. In the meantime, my husband had arrived to console me. My daughters retreated upstairs to my sister, to the aunt they loved, and returned to tell me that she doesn't want me to be angry with her, but that she just needs to be sure.

When I arrived back on my dad's floor, the entire family was gathered outside the ICU, my brothers and sister in front. Everyone else waited quietly on the fringes as I joined my siblings. It was clear that there had been much discussion in my absence about what had taken place. I looked at the faces of my brothers and sister splotched with grief and a quiet resignation. One by one I called their names and one by one they said they were ready. We notified the doctor, who brought us back to a small room where he stood with us and explained Dad's condition.

For the first time, my sister and brothers were hearing the words "vegetable," "no hope for recovery," "a good decision." I was relieved and ached powerfully for them. My sister wanted just enough morphine to make him comfortable and no more. The young doctor assured us of that as well as giving Dad oxygen when the ventilator was removed to make him more comfortable. I signed the forms authorizing removing life support, and after the doctor left, we held hands and prayed, my sister and me crying and our two strong brothers supporting us. I thanked her for a courageous "letting go," and in her face I saw the realization and the agony of all the future moments now lost to her. The promise of all that she had wished for with Dad would go with him. Gone now was every bit of anger and resentment as we supported each other in the love that has held us for a lifetime.

Mom went alone to Dad's bedside, forgave him, and released him. The grandchildren and our spouses said their goodbyes. We all waited outside as the life support was removed—the feeding tubes, the antibiotic, the ventilator—and replaced with an oxygen mask and morphine for comfort. In that time, we planned a service (the Catholic priest who had given Dad the last rites and prayed with us previously was not available). We gave the first reading, a prayer that Dad had said each day, to Mom because, as we told her, without her, we would not exist. We gave the second reading to Dad's companion. As we gathered around his bedside, each of us laying a hand on him, we prayed and prayed and prayed, building a path of prayers for him to the other side. We prayed until we were spent. Dad labored to breathe, his heart strong, and he held on. He was a healthy dying man.

The next day, he was still working hard, and we retired to his apartment leaving Hennie to watch over him. We worked together packing and sharing his belongings, generous and solicitous with each other in the process. We rented a truck that my daughter and her husband agreed to drive back to Maryland so that everyone who wanted something of Dad's would have it. It was a long long day and we were all tired and hungry. Hennie called from the hospital to say that Dad's breathing was erratic. I spoke with the nurse who assured us that we could have dinner before returning, that he was in no danger of dying soon, but that they were moving him out of ICU to a semi-private room. One daughter had already left, and others had flights early the next morning. My sister and younger brother and I would stay until the last breath. We separated into three cars for dinner and I assured my younger brother, who was going with some others, that there was no need to hurry back to the hospital. I went with my sister, niece, and nephew to a fast food restaurant, and we all ate on the way back to the hospital. It was late at night so we entered through the Emergency Room entrance and wound our way through the mammoth complex to Dad's new room.

Upon entering, my sister exclaimed, "Where's Dad?" I replied, "He's right there." No, she said, that's not Dad. I walked over to him with a dawning as I touched his face. "Oh my God," I cried. "Dad's dead, he's gone!"

My niece, so used now to my praying over him, immediately said, "Patsy pray!" We held hands and prayed him to Jesus, all of us crying as the male nurse ran in to exclaim, "You weren't supposed to find him! It only happened five minutes ago and I didn't have a chance to call the family," he said, "I'm so sorry." As he was apologizing, Dad's roommate was freaking out in the next bed, affronted by Dad's death right there in his room.

Finally, it was quiet and we stayed with him. Our younger brother arrived prepared to be distraught over not being there and was comforted to know that none of us was there for his last breath. We believed that Dad, not wanting him excluded, and sensing us leaving our car and winding our way to him, hurried up his dying so that Butch would not be left out. We were grateful for his sensitivity. It had taken thirty-two hours after removing the ventilator for Dad's body to tire of breathing.

We left our younger brother, Butch, to be with Dad and walked to the nurse's station to make our calls to the rest of the family, contact the funeral director, and wait for the morgue transporter. We wanted to be with Dad throughout.

Cremations in Florida are very inexpensive. It must have something to do with volume business. They also have a forty-eight hour wait before a cremation is done. The crematory we selected agreed to fax us the forms in the morning for authorization and information that we would then fax back to them with payment. The total came to $516, which included filing a death notice, mailing his remains to my home in Maryland, and six death certificates. The crematory informed me that only the one needed for insurance purposes would require listing the cause of death. I also had a strange telephone encounter with another crematory's agent who quoted me twice as much as the one we selected. When I inquired about the disparity in price for the same service, he growled that if I didn't like it I could take my business elsewhere. It was an unpleasant encounter in an otherwise pleasing relationship with the hospital's personnel.

As we waited in the hall for the nurses to attend to Dad, I looked over at Butch, whose hand raised to his head recalled another young son's salute for his father. I remarked in kind, "Oh no, we'll have to call you Butch-Butch from now on." But I said it tenderly seeing his silent grief. I then joined the nurses where my father lay naked on the bed and I helped to wrap him in the white plastic sheet that we taped tightly around his body. I began to appreciate the Jewish and Muslim customs of shrouding and felt a spiritual connectedness. I watched as the sheet obliterated his human features, reducing him to an unrecognizable embryo. I gently massaged his heart through the sheet as I imagined my Dad moving away from us, whited out in light, and reentering the birth canal, traveling through to the womb whence he came, to be birthed out the other side.

When I rejoined my family in the hall, and as our father and grandfather was wheeled out and down the long hallway, my brother first saluted solemnly, and then my nephew, and my niece followed, and then my sister, and my husband, and finally me. We saluted the coming in and the going out, as our Dad and Granddad traveled the long hall, and as he disappeared from our view and rounded the next turn of his life.

# What Life Means to Me

It is important for your family and your healthcare advocate to know the things you value. What makes life worth living? These thoughts will help them to support your wishes if you are unable to speak for yourself.

*In every parting there is an image of death.*
George Eliot
(1819–1880)

# Fred's Story

In first grade, I decided that I wanted to be a veterinarian, in large part due to my love of animals. When I was in high school, my parents wisely arranged for me to have a summer job in an animal hospital. My first day was remarkable and exciting. Soon after walking in the door, I was thrust into the small operating room where I assisted in the spaying of an enormous Great Dane. The dog was asleep on her back on the operating table, her legs splayed out, each one extending well off the table and into the corners of the small room. To get around the table to where the doctor (who was elbow-deep in Great Dane) wanted me, I had to duck under the dog's legs.

After a week or so, I grew accustomed to the day-to-day operation of the hospital. I participated in examinations, surgeries, and, of course, cleaning cages. One thing I never got used to was the death of an animal, whether it happened through illness or injury or euthanasia to end suffering. Every dog or cat that melted into my arms as it exhaled its last breath left an indelible mark on me.

I can still actually see some of these marks today, nearly fifteen years later. One day, an owner brought his cat to the office. The cat was ill again, the third time in as many months. The owner had grown weary of the veterinary bills and constant attention the cat required and asked that we put it down. In the back room, I held the struggling, angry cat as the doctor prepared the injection. In an instant, the cat swiped my right index finger with its paw. Bleeding all over my white gown, I cursed the cat as the doctor injected the poison. In an instant, the cat was dead. I still have the scar inflicted on me by the only creature that I had ever wished dead, a reminder of an instance of cruelty that I still regret. I like to think that the cat, which an autopsy later revealed was riddled with malignant tumors, got the last word.

It was the death of another cat that left most of us at the hospital in tears. The small, gentle, elderly tabby was a frequent visitor to the hospital that summer, sometimes spending a week at a time with us while one symptom or another of the illness that was gradually killing it manifested itself. One morning toward the end of the summer, the doctor telephoned the owner, gently informed her that the cat's organs were failing, and that it was time to consider putting the cat to sleep to avoid any suffering.

That afternoon, the entire family appeared to bid farewell to their friend. They were losing a family member, one that had been around since before the birth of their two children, who were now teenagers. They spent over an hour in an examining room alone with the cat. They had fashioned a small casket from a red toolbox. The small pillow on the bottom was covered with flower petals, and on the inside of the lid were photographs of the family.

I did not become a veterinarian. But, in hindsight, it occurs to me that I learned a lot about death from the summer at the animal hospital and that, generally speaking, children have a tremendous opportunity to learn important lessons about life and death from their cherished pets. I learned that every living creature is born and ultimately dies, and that these two simple facts cannot be avoided. I learned that there are few distinctions between being with a dying pet and with a dying person, that sometimes we can be full of love and compassion and sometimes stingy with our generosity. I also learned that death with dignity is something that we strive to provide for in our pets and yet . . .

# Helpful Information for Choosing My Healthcare Agent

The Durable Power of Attorney for Healthcare is a legal document allowing you to name another person (a healthcare agent) to make medical decisions if you become unable to make them for yourself, whatever your condition.

This person may be your spouse, adult child, a relative, or friend—someone who is able to lobby on your behalf. Choose someone who can talk to doctors, collect, sift, and synthesize information and make decisions. Your agent should be someone who knows you well, knows your values, and knows what you would want in whatever medical crisis you face. It is advisable to choose an alternate should your first choice be unable to act under this document. Your agent should also have a copy of your Living Will.

This Medical Power of Attorney, sometimes contained in the Living Will as one document, can authorize your agent to make general medical decisions on your behalf or it can set forth specific decisions as outlined by you. It becomes effective when two physicians, including your attending physician, certify that you lack the capacity and understanding to make meaningful healthcare decisions on your own behalf. Your agent then is obligated to follow your instructions when making decisions for you.

Now consider the questions below and choose your healthcare agent.

# Safeguarding Your Wishes

Whom do you trust?

Who is the person whose counsel you respect?

Who can access and process information effectively and make informed decisions?

Whom do you consider a strong and effective communicator and mediator?

Who knows you well enough to advocate on your behalf?

Who perseveres in difficult circumstances?

*That person is your healthcare spokesperson or agent.*

---

In a medical crisis, that voice becomes yours to underscore the wishes you have outlined in your Living Will. Although it is suggested that your healthcare agent not be a person who benefits financially from your estate, do not let this deter you from choosing the one person who meets your criteria of love, trust, and comfort.

So, whom do you trust with your life?

Answer here _____

Good! Now go to page 157 and complete your Advance Directives. You may also secure these forms for the state in which you live by writing to Partnership for Caring, Inc., a Choice in Dying, 1035 30th Street, NW, Washington, D.C. 20007, 1-800-989-9455, www.partnershipforcaring.org, or visit any hospital in your state and ask for Advance Directives forms.

# Free to Be

Wow! That was a really important piece of work you have just completed. Important for two reasons: When we start the process of final arrangements, we are starting a conversation about death; and when we talk about and plan for our own death, it frees us up to live our life, fully and without anxiety.

Historically, I have always welcomed and dreaded vacations, especially if they involved air travel. I wasn't so much afraid of flying as I was afraid of dying. More so because I had done zero about protecting my children, providing for them, and arming them with information that would lessen their burden should I not return. I felt anxious, reckless, and irresponsible, and before every vacation would hurriedly deliver a handwritten will to my children or (can you believe this?) a Post-it™ note stating that I was leaving them all of my worldly possessions. Finally, before my last trip, my daughter declared, "That's it, Mom! No more Post-it™ notes!" I dared not leave this time without doing as she had begged so many times before.

I called a lawyer/friend who was user-friendly and who came to our home, gathered the necessary information, and delivered to us the day before our departure our Advance Medical Directives, Durable Power of Attorney, and Last Will and Testament, which I then entrusted to my daughter.

She cried then as she always does when saying goodbye, but this time there was more relief than anxiety in her tears. That hurdle having been overcome, I was gifted with the most relaxed, the most free, the most joyous vacation I had ever experienced. Facing the possibility of my dying with a plan in place freed me to live every wonderful moment of my trip without fear and without anxiety.

# planning and attending your own memorial service: the last dance

Even though I walk through the valley of
the shadow of death,
I fear no evil; for thou art with me . . .

Psalms 23:4

*I*n a scene from the film, *Dirty Dancing*, Patrick Swayze's character
locked dance positions with "Baby" and instructed, "This is my dance
space, and this is your dance space."

Attending your own memorial service is like that. As dancers we
can move with and among each other, but always we inhabit our own
spaces. Nowhere is that more evident than when one of us is dying,
when one of us is "going home." And that is as it should be. The "last
dance" together allows us the space to say our goodbyes while still
holding one another.

For some, that space might be a small gathering; for others, a full-
scale party replete with all of the accoutrements of gaiety. For Julia, it
was a sacredly planned service in our church that lasted longer than
planned and made us laugh until we cried, and made us cry until we
could all laugh again.

The idea for this event surfaced when, as her friends, we mused
about how we might honor her life after she had been diagnosed with
terminal brain cancer. She was forty-nine years old. Slowly, it dawned
on us that the best way was one where Julia was present and could
participate. When approached with the idea, she was hesitant at first,
believing it might prove too sad. But she trusted us, and that trust
overcame her reservations. So we set about structuring the event, feeling
our way, having no models to guide us. Our minister was on sabbatical
that year, and it was left to us as her faith community to respond.

We structured the event to begin with a potluck luncheon, followed by a service. Julia participated in the planning by choosing the hymns, scriptural readings, and poems that were meaningful to her. Others chose songs that spoke of her substantial being. I had wanted Julia to tell her own story in her own words, but as the day approached and the cancer stole away her voice, she asked that I deliver it instead. But how to do that?

I first interviewed Julia, her family, her friends and colleagues until the tapestry that was Julia revealed itself. So compelling was her story that the night before the service, when I sat down to write, it flowed seamlessly onto paper. I felt divinely guided and knew enough about agape moments to get out of the way and let it come.

On the day of celebration, my children and friends filled colorful balloons with helium and anchored them to chairs and railings so they floated in the sky. Friends, family, and colleagues streamed in carrying all manner of food and drink, each greeting Julia and showering her with love. We had our meal together, she smiling and crying and laughing out loud, and all of us laughing and crying with her.

One person walked into this scene objecting to the premise with a pointed question. "Whose idea was this," she demanded as the pianist played "Amazing Grace." "This is too sad," she said, "I won't be able to speak!" But she did speak, taking her turn at the open mike, along with scores of others who shared their experience of Julia with us and to her.

I am uncomfortable speaking to large groups. I do it, but I am always nervous. This day, however, as I was guided in the writing of Julia's story, so was I guided in the delivering. The telling of it brought tears, smiles, and laughter. Filled to the brim with every conceivable emotion, Julia stayed with it all. I knew even without asking as the day unfolded that her trust in us had been rewarded. She watched the video of that day, of her "last dance" with us, almost to the end when, six short weeks later, she died.

If any of you are fortunate enough to have this time together, don't miss the chance for a last dance; it lends untold richness to the end of life. Call it "A Living Tribute," "A Life's Celebration," "A Living Memorial," whatever you wish. Ask permission of the dying person and involve him or her in the process. If the conditions are favorable, seize the opportunity and don't be afraid, because I believe that whenever we enter a sacred space with a full and loving heart, our words and actions are always rendered perfect!

# an introduction to hospice

## Reclaiming Our Rights

Separated from birth by bright lights
  altering drugs, cold sterile rooms,
    masked and cloaked attendants,
we seek to reclaim our birthright,
  with midwives, studied breaths,
    in warm rooms, eyes wide open.
What was schooled out of us,
      reschooled in us,
  freeing us from the isolation of birthing,
  linking us to families present
  in joyful celebration of the coming in!

Separated from death by bright lights
  altering drugs, cold sterile rooms,
    masked and cloaked attendants,
we seek to reclaim our deathright,
  with hospitable helpers, studied breaths,
  in warm rooms, eyes wide open.
What was schooled out of us,
      reschooled in us,
  freeing us from the isolation of dying
  linking us to families present
    and past
  in sweet surrender to the going out.

✌

*How we care for the most ill, infirm and advanced elderly is the central moral challenge confronting the baby boom generation. In great measure, this will be the issue by which history will judge us.*

                                        Ira R. Byock, M.D.
                                        *Dying Well*

# Linda's Story

When I agreed to take care of my mother, it was an automatic response on my part. She had been diagnosed with terminal lung cancer thirteen months before, and had undergone chemotherapy during that time. She had lived completely on her own, and except for a few sick days, had lived a fairly normal life. But the time had come when the cancer was getting the best of her and she could no longer live by herself. Having her with me in those last three months of her life was something I wanted to do, especially because she never wanted to end up in a nursing home.

Mom was never really incapacitated until toward the end. She just gradually got weaker. She was mobile enough for us to go on a cruise together, to visit her hometown, and to take short trips around town. She could bathe and dress herself almost until the last few weeks. It never really dawned on me that I was agreeing to watch her die by degrees every day.

We actually had a very good life until then. This particular year, however, brought with it a series of losses and near losses. It seemed that all we would experience of death and loss would be compressed into this one year of our lives.

They came in waves: Between January and October of that year we had experienced one crisis after another that finally ended with my mother's death. First, two of my children were in separate car crashes that they miraculously walked away from. Then my husband's mother died after a ten-week illness, after which we learned that my mother's lung cancer had spread to her brain. Then two friends died suddenly of heart attacks. Shortly after that, I spent five days as an outpatient receiving intravenous antibiotic treatments for a poisonous spider bite. Then my husband's brother-in-law died suddenly of a heart attack. Throughout all of these crises, I kept reminding myself that we could have lost our children, too, but didn't. It felt strangely reassuring; and I was taking care of Mom.

I wasn't intimate with my mother. She was somewhat critical and could injure with her words, so we kept a respectful distance. Mom, however, respected my husband's presence and was always on her best behavior around him. That helped to ease any major eruptions. Plus, I think that either she mellowed from the cancer's effect on her brain, from her closeness to death, or both.

Mom and I never talked about death. Even now I can't talk to my husband or children about it, or talk about burial plots. I just couldn't do that! It would be too scary. We just never talked about those things as a family.

I remember that the first oncologist who diagnosed her cancer would not give us any information. Then we switched to another oncologist, who was very informative although somewhat optimistic—he said she could live five years with chemo treatments—the statistics say one year. This was actually 16 months before she died.

I didn't bring in hospice until seven days before she died, because I didn't really need it, and I wanted to continue with as normal a life for her as possible. We didn't really know that much about it, but our doctor recommended hospice be brought in at that time. Before that I was managing well, I thought. I had taken a six-month leave of absence from my job to take care of Mom. My husband and our two teenage children were also at home and helped out some, and my sister was also available to take care of her.

Hospice, in the short time it was with us, provided a respite. The hospice people showed me how to live with her until she died. I think prior to that we were just living each day as if she weren't dying. At the end, she just stayed in her room and basically said: "Leave me alone; don't bother me!" So I didn't want to bother her. From the health aide who bathed and dressed her and managed to get her to smile, to the nurse who cared for her, to the volunteer who sat with her two days before she died so that I could keep an appointment, I just can't say enough about their level of care. They just came and did their thing, and it was all wonderful. They did all the things that I wasn't trained to do and wasn't emotionally fit to do—bathing, dressing, changing the bed with Mom in it, prescribing and delivering medicine, and advising us what to expect the next day. I could not have kept Mom at home her last week without the help of hospice.

Mom died, at the age of seventy-seven, on a sunny Saturday afternoon, after being bedridden for five days and noncommunicative for about three days. I think the morphine that she had started for pain four days before her death helped in her transition from life to death. It was peaceful for her, and her close family was there, including a special niece. The hospice nurse was called and arrived almost within the hour, pronounced her dead, and summoned the undertaker whom they had already alerted. A big chapter in my life was over, and I closed it feeling that I had made Mom's death as easy for her as I could have. With the help of hospice, I was able to keep her from the institution that she had dreaded since the days of my childhood.

People asked me whether it bothered me to have someone die in my home, and it really didn't. I think the hospital bed that was brought in made it seem less intrusive, almost as if it provided a degree of separation. Maybe we should have had hospice in sooner, but, again, I thought I was managing. Having a year of so many unplanned things happening, I didn't dare plan anything.

We survived it. However, today I just don't know if I could bear one more crisis. I don't know what that would do to me. So we are enjoying this time now, where nothing traumatic is happening.

*After the first death there is no other.*
Dylan Thomas
(1914–1953)

Your grandparents and great grandparents would remember what it was like years ago when generations lived together under the same roof. When babies and the aged coexisted, when we did not see the wrinkles and the deterioration of aging, but welcomed the ample arms surrounding us, the soft bosom to snuggle into, the twinkling crinkling smile, and the toothy laugh, the weathered hands that guided us, and the earthy scent that spelled security. And they would remember the seamless line between birth and death. They would remember learning about both from being there, up close and personal, the smell of life bursting forth and the smell of death beckoning us home again. They would remember how they came to know and to accept life in all of its transformations. They came to understand the impermanence of being by their familiarity with death. When the shock of it came, they accepted it and moved on . . .

Today, with families scattered about, and with the advent of retirement villages, assisted living, and nursing homes, autumn lives are farther and farther removed, taking with them the smell of death from us. We are lost to this most valuable experience, which we can only get from being with the dying.

Hospices, of which there are now 3,000 in the United States, serve to bridge that gap by recreating a nurturing environment for the dying and their families.

# Hospice—A New Way of Seeing and Being

Hospice is a way of shaking hands with death, of saying: "Welcome, old friend. I haven't known you, yet I've always known you, knew you'd be coming for me someday."

The word *hospice* means an inn for travelers. Today a hospice stay marks the beginning of the last leg of the journey home. To choose hospice care is to choose a resting place, a place of renewal, an unencumbered breathing space before our last breath. In that space and time, you, the patient, and your family are treated with great and special care.

Hospice care differs from traditional medical treatment in several ways:

+ The goal is not to cure but to enable patients to carry on in an alert, pain-free manner. Hospice does not try to slow down the dying process, nor does it try to hasten it.
+ Hospice treats the whole person, not just the disease. Patients are assisted with spiritual, emotional, and practical matters.

- Hospice includes the family in the patient care and a team of professionals. This team consists of a doctor, nurse, social worker, home health aide, chaplain, and volunteer.
- Hospice has programs that specifically help family members, such as caregiver support groups and bereavement counseling. It can provide advice and aid to caregivers whose health and finances may suffer from caring for a seriously ill family member.
- Hospice honors the patient's wishes—the patient's preferences form the foundation of the care plan.
- Hospice provides (usually) free bereavement counseling, either individually or in groups, for one year after the death. This can be a vital lifeline for dealing with and healing from a death.
- One little known fact—if you are in hospice home care, Medicare pays for five days' respite care in an inpatient hospice facility, which is a tremendous help to families exhausted by caregiving.

The wonder of hospice is that, from within this cadre of professionals and lay volunteers, comes a soft, steady outpouring of love that gently supports families and their loved ones through very difficult times. I've seen it happen and each time was awed by these "soft" professionals. I've seen them gently bridge patients' and family members' resistance to death with compassion.

# Eligibility for Hospice

At present, anyone with a terminal disease who no longer responds to or chooses curative treatments, and who is estimated to have six months or less to live by two physicians, is eligible for hospice. Hospice care is available in hospitals, your own home, nursing homes, retirement communities, and other long-term residential care facilities. Whatever program you choose, the emphasis is always on palliative—pain-free and comfortable—care.

# Paying for Hospice

There are approximately 3,000 hospices in the United States, over two-thirds of which are Medicare certified. Most services are fully or partially covered by Medicare, Medicaid, HMOs, or private insurers, providing a doctor has estimated that the patient has six months or less to live. Check your private insurance to see if it covers inpatient and home hospice care. In a residential hospice, which may be in a homelike setting or on a hospital floor, room and board usually are paid by the patient or by private insurance. Under certain strict parameters, Medicare or private insurance pays for room and board for certain acute conditions.

# Deciding on Hospice

You might decide for yourself that you are ready for hospice care. Referrals can also be made by your family members, doctors, other health professionals, friends, and clergy. In most cases, however, your primary care physician certifies and approves the need for hospice care. Then, one must go through admission screening as a condition of being accepted into hospice, and admission must be approved by the hospice physician.

Like other final arrangements, it is best to familiarize yourself with hospice before the need occurs. Find out what hospice care is available in your area. Some places still do not have hospice care; others provide a variety of options. Do your research. Check out the public library, talk with people who have used hospice, talk with your doctor or insurance carrier, or contact the Hospice Foundation of America, 2001 S Street, NW, #300, Washington, DC 20009, 1-800-854-3402 or log on its Web site http://www.hospicefoundation.org

It is important to note that choosing hospice is not a once-and-forever decision. You may cancel the hospice service at any time and return to standard Medicare coverage and hospice can be selected again at a later time. But don't wait until the very end, when it can only offer brink-of-death care. Those who benefit the most from hospice get the services as early as possible. Don't let your own fear of death deny you the help available through hospice. Regard it as another rite of passage, a crossing-over space sprinkled with richness and promising a new way of seeing and being.

That said, the best way to learn about hospice and to share in the dying experience is to become a hospice volunteer (read Anne's story below).

✂

> *Everything flows and nothing stays.*
> Heraclitus
> (c. 540–480 b.c.)

# Anne's Story
# On Being a Hospice Volunteer

When people learn that I am a hospice volunteer, the reactions are often something like this: "Oh, how wonderful you are doing that. I never could." "I would rather focus on living than on dying. Doesn't it make you feel rather morbid?" "I really don't know anyone who has died and wouldn't know how to handle it. Thank goodness I don't have to!"

As for me, I had rarely been around a person in the last stages of dying, and I wouldn't have known what to do either! That is precisely why I decided to check out what it would be like to volunteer. I'm at the age where I know for a fact that I will soon be losing family members and friends, and the thought of that sobers me for several reasons. Obviously, I knew I would experience deep grief, but another fear was that I wouldn't know how to deal with this person during the dying process.

So I applied to be a volunteer with our local hospice chapter. First, I completed an application and submitted the names of three references. This was followed by an interview with the volunteer coordinator who assured me that after the training, if I decided that this wasn't for me, I was under no obligation to be a volunteer. They believe that just by offering the training to those who might be interested, they were educating the community.

Our training group ranged in age from the late twenties into the mid-seventies and represented women and men from a variety of backgrounds and careers. We were all quite still and somber that first Friday night as we waited for our coordinator and trainer to start the session. Eight weeks later, after approximately forty hours, we were intimately aware of our own issues and needs with regard to dying. We had also gained a sense of the commonality of our fears and an understanding of how to help people effectively during the final months of their lives. We had also learned lots of very practical information.

In the weeks following the training session, we each had a follow-up meeting with the coordinator to evaluate the training and to determine whether we still wanted to volunteer. I did. I have the right of refusal for any patient for any reason. I was assured that I would never be on my own because hospice help was only as far away as the telephone. We are also part of a team of medical, social, and psychological professionals in which the volunteer also is treated as a professional.

A few days later I received a call from the coordinator saying there was a case for me if I felt I wanted to handle it after learning the facts of the situation. I did and, as I always do the first time going to meet a new patient, I got completely lost. It's probably nervousness, wondering what the situation will be like. But so far, once there, it has always been fine for me. The excellent training prepared me well.

My patients usually dictate what my time will be like. Some days I sit and listen, other days there are spirited, interactive conversations. We might share a meal together, I might relieve a caregiver who goes off to do other things, or I might be used to run errands.

Sometimes a friendship is made with a caregiver that continues after the death of the patient. These after-death meetings stem from the common experience of being there together for their loved one. Talking together about the deceased comes easily then and seems to offer comfort and peace for them and closure for me.

What have I learned from my hospice work? Some patients are easier or more likeable than others. Sometimes I feel more needed than at other times. Sometimes I look forward to going and other times not. But, always, when I leave my hospice patient, my own life seems richer than it had been, more purposeful, and I feel more alive. So you see? Hospice is not just about dying, it's about living too.

*We shall not cease from exploration*
*And the end of all our exploring*
*Will be to arrive where we started*
*And know the place for the first time.*

T. S. Eliot
(1888–1965)

# George's Story

I have already faced the fact that I am going to die. I am an only child. My father died of complications from liver cancer when I was twenty-one. He was sixty-three. My mother died four years later of a heart attack at age sixty-two.

I was very close to my grandfather, who died four years after my parents. He introduced me to carpentry, and I remember at five or six years of age when he would set up boards for me to hammer together. My grandfather had bone cancer and wanted to die at home. However, he had dementia and was at times delirious, so I was unable to care for him at home. We had to put him in a nursing home—a place he did not want to be. He stayed for ten days, and I visited him every day. On the ninth day, I found him sitting up in bed, with eyes wide open saying, "You've got to get me out of here!" He opened his hand to show me a combination of pills that he had been storing, pills that distorted his perception and his consciousness.

I found a private agency, a home care nursing service, which provided a live-in and allowed him to stay in his own home until he died. I wasn't aware of hospice then. My closeness to my grandfather and my experiences with death made me want to share the experiences of dying people, so I became a hospice volunteer.

As a volunteer, I am seldom with patients who can interact and am therefore unable to explore with them what they might be going through. Dementia patients seldom recognize what is around them. Mostly my presence is enveloped in silence or one-sided conversations. Once, a patient drifted in and out of an ongoing dialogue with me.

In the absence of a verbal interaction, I try to form a spiritual connection with my patients, one that allows a sense of feeling beyond their physical experience. I might stay fifteen minutes or an hour and a half, but each time I strive for that spiritual connectedness.

My daughter calls me a Zen Buddhist Catholic Naturalist. I see God in squirrels, in trees, in people. My Catholic upbringing gave me a spiritual grounding, allowing me to question with an open mind. I go camping once or twice a year and I meditate every day to re-establish a spiritual connection. I try not to generalize about people. I believe that we are put here to love every person unconditionally.

I believe that any path to God and the spirit is a good path. Choosing a religion really is choosing a path upon which you can pursue God. Ultimately, all of our answers have to be personal answers, coming from our hearts.

My wish is that I could have known at age seven or eight what I know now. The real reason that hospice exists is that there is such a lack of early planning for death, a recognition at an early age of death—not in a morbid negative way, but in a positive light. I am a diabetic, a condition with possible long-term complications. This past summer, I was on IV medication for three months from a foot wound that would not heal. I told my children that I wouldn't be here forever. Their response was, "Don't worry Dad, you'll be here for a long time." Then I tell them that *they* won't be here forever, and to find peace within themselves. Talk to your children about death when they are happy.

The recognition that I am a spiritual being having a human experience makes me tingle, understanding that this is the truth of life, and death. There is continuity no matter what, unless you can say that you were never created. Voltaire says that it is no less inconceivable to be born twice than to be born once.

The Tibetans understand the preciousness of every day, that every day could be a last day. They give thanks for the morning and at night turn their teacups upside down when they go to bed. Tomorrow, or the next life, is their belief. Whichever comes first.

❧

# Some Thoughts on Dying

Making arrangements for leaving this world allows me a measure of
closure. However, practical matters are only the beginning. The process
of sharing my concerns and wishes with family and friends inevitably
brings up the potential loss and attendant emotions. It is then that I
begin to examine my relationships and am moved to speak from the
heart. In this way, every future encounter suggests a "last encounter," and
I am left with a sense of completeness with each person with whom I
interact. Talking about death makes me aware of my own spirituality
and level of preparedness. However, I believe that dying itself will
transform me again in a way that the "not yet" cannot. But, I would hope
that, after the practical and concrete measures of my living will are
applied, I would be surrounded with love and be released in love. I want
my family and friends to feel useful and necessary in helping me to cross
over into death. I want us to be partners in the dance, each of us
knowing we will become even more accessible to the other in another
realm. I want to die with a smile on my face and in my heart and know,
too, that you are also smiling.

# My Own Thoughts
## on How I Would Like to Die

*Strength without hands to smite;*
*Love that endures for a breath;*
*Night, the shadow of light,*
*And life, the shadow of death.*

Algernon Charles Swinburne
(1837–1909)

# Marilyn's Story

It had been a very hot summer. I was looking forward to beginning a new school year, in a new school, in a new town. Instead, I lay in a hospital bed, the upper half of my body in an oxygen tent, barely able to breathe. Asthma, pneumonia, collapsed lungs with complications had converged to leave me a lifeless form. I was a slim girl of ten years, but now I was nothing but skin stretched over bones.

Was I dying? What was dying anyway? What happens when a person dies? Where did a person go? Did that mean that I wouldn't be able to get new school shoes at Kinney's? I wanted those black, slip-on leather shoes with the little ties. I thought all this while unable to breathe.

An attendant came and lifted me from my bed and strapped me to a gurney. An oxygen mask was placed on my face. Everyone was working quickly. Where was I going? I was already in a hospital! No one had time to tell me, not even my father, the physician.

I was wheeled out into the hot September night, a still night, as the ambulance door was opened and I was placed inside. A still night as my parents took their seats up front. A still night broken only by the soft-spoken voice of the attendant monitoring the oxygen. He spoke of how it feels to go so fast through the night, how the bottom of the ambulance felt as if it were going to drop out. He promised he would be there for the entire trip. I felt his care and tenderness. He explained to me that we had a long way to go and that halfway through the trip he would be going to a second tank of oxygen. He said not to be afraid.

The stillness of the night broke with the frightening blare of the siren as the ambulance started up and we whizzed through the streets.

It seemed as if the whole world stopped for me then, and I felt oddly special. At the university hospital I was placed in an oxygen tent in the intensive care unit. There were no visitors except my parents. My brother, the only one who made me laugh, came once and then went off to Harvard for the start of his freshman year. My illness was a mystery to all.

We were a prominent family in the community, a family that seemed perfect from the outside. Perfection was the model, in comportment and in achievements. There was no room for messiness. And I was slowly dying.

Thirty-one years later my father lay dying in a hospital. For eight weeks I visited almost daily. Too weak to move or speak, he needed help with everything. I assisted when I could, shaving him, brushing his teeth, feeding him, and at times just holding his hand. All of the feelings and memories of my earlier years came back. I realized that I had survived the near death of my body and my soul. I was very proud, very joyful, that, in spite of those years, I could be there fully for my father. The sadness that remained, however, was that after a lifetime, he was incapable of giving me what I needed the most. He passed from my life on a steamy hot August morning, his opportunity forever lost, and the pain of this etched deeply in my heart.

# donating organs and tissues

You may break, you may shatter the vase, if you will,
But the scent of the roses will hang round it still.

Thomas Moore
(1779–1852)

When death comes, it is our spirit, the prize of our being, that journeys on. It is the one thing we take with us. Our bodies, well designed for this world, would not suit us in our travels to the beyond. When death comes, they no longer have any value to us. But these bodies can become a treasure trove for those we leave behind.

These "treasures" can be our parting gifts. They can be the gift of sight, of breath, the heart that lives on, and the myriad other human components that sustain a life.

Donating these gifts to others is the ultimate in giving and the difference between buried treasure and a living memorial. This is what it means to be an organ donor, a giver of life. It is by design, sacred music, the universal language of love.

## Facts You Should Know about Organ and Tissue Donation*

- You must be free of active cancer, AIDS, HIV, and other communicable diseases.
- Kidneys, hearts, livers, lungs, pancreas, and intestines can be donated. Skin, bone, veins, soft tissue, heart valves, corneas, and eyes can be donated

---

*Source: Transplant Resource Center of Maryland.

- Organs are removed only after the donor has been declared legally brain dead.
- Tissue can be donated only after the heart has stopped.
- Organs are never removed if a family member objects, even if the dying person has stated otherwise. For this reason, it is important to discuss your wishes with your family.
- There is no cost to the donor family for organ/tissue recovery–related charges. In the United States, it is illegal for anyone to buy or sell a body or any part of a body.
- There is no change in the appearance of the body after donation that would interfere with an open casket funeral.
- Donor cards are available through recognized donor procurement organizations. In most states, donors can also say yes to donation when obtaining or renewing a driver's license. A donor form is provided for you on the next page.
- Donor cards should be completed and carried with you at all times.
- You may include donor decisions in your living will.
- The principles and practice of organ/tissue donation are approved by all major religious denominations. Discuss any concerns with your spiritual advisor.

# Organ/Tissue Donation Instructions

I direct that if I am brain dead, an anatomical gift be offered on my behalf to a patient in need of an organ or tissue transplant. If a transplant occurs, I want artificial heart/lung support devices to be continued on my behalf only until organ or tissue suitability of the patient is confirmed and organ or tissue recovery has taken place.

## SIGNATURE OF DECLARANT

By signing below, I indicate that I am emotionally and mentally competent to make these Organ/Tissue Donation Instructions and that I understand their purpose and effect.

Signature of Declarant                                    Date

## SIGNATURE OF WITNESSES

The declarant signed or acknowledged signing these Organ/Tissue Donation Instructions in my presence, and, based upon my personal observation, appears to be a competent individual.

First Witness Signature                                    Date

Second Witness Signature                                   Date

*If you press me to say why I loved him,*
*I can say no more than it was because*
*he was he and I was I.*

Michel Eyquem de Montaigne
(1533–1592)

# Morris's Story

The idea that Ruth and I might donate our brains to
medical research was first suggested by her doctor in the
geriatric neurology department of Francis Scott Key
Hospital within the Johns Hopkins University
Medical System.

Almost immediately after Ruth was diagnosed
with Alzheimer's, she was invited to become a subject in a research
project on the effectiveness of an experimental drug. Sometime
thereafter her doctor also asked Ruth to donate her brain. Since Ruth
was already relying on me in such judgments (she had given me durable
power of attorney covering health and medical matters), I was party to
the conversation. Ruth and I agreed that she would approve donation of
her brain to the doctor's research team on her death.

Still later, someone at the hospital said that normal brains were
needed for comparison with those of Alzheimer's patients. Knowing a
bit about research design, I asked whether the normal brains should be
those of siblings of the Alzheimer's patient (certain genes being
suspected at least as partial culprits in the causation of Alzheimer's).
The response was that any old normal brain would do, whereupon I
volunteered to ask my friend Jim if he would join me in beefing up the
brain bank. I took the eager acceptance as evidence that Jim and I both
have normal brains.

This agreement having been reached, I was given some instructions
about how to provide an official record of intent to donate and was put
in touch with the Maryland Anatomy Board, through which the
donation would have to be made. The board, in turn, asked if we would

donate other organs suitable for transplant (as distinguished from research). I indicated our willingness to do so.

I duly executed the required document and gave copies to my HMO, my attorney, and the Anatomy Board. Then I learned that I would have to fill out documents again at the time of Ruth's death and have my designee do so for me when I die. These forms were also provided to me.

What I did not understand as I was arranging for her donation and subsequent cremation was that the organs for transplant would have to be removed before Ruth died. This news was a major shock, coming as it did so long after my original discussion with the Anatomy Board staff member, and not discovered until the week before Ruth's death when we realized that her stroke made it unavoidable that she would die within a few hours to a few days. Removing organs before death would kill her before the natural effects of the stroke, it seemed to me. I was not about to authorize proactively terminating her life.

The spokesperson at the Anatomy Board explained that brain death can precede the heart's closing down. But I did not know whether a diagnosis of irreversible coma was the same as a diagnosis of brain death, and it seemed a bit ghoulish to be consulting Ruth's doctor on that question at that time. So I cancelled the permission to donate the organs for transplant. This sudden decision may have been a disservice to some person in need of an immediate transplant, but I was in no mood to decide otherwise without substantial time to think through a different choice.*

By the time Ruth breathed her last, I had been assigned hospice support by my medical plan and the hospital. All of our children were in the house or close by when Ruth died. The hospice nurse was informed a few minutes after Ruth's death and was there when the funeral home person arrived.

Since we were deep into a weekend when she died, we had to call the morgue and Johns Hopkins Hospital to find out whether the body needed to be delivered to them Sunday evening for proper preservation. The hospital asked that we do so promptly. Locating the proper person took several phone calls, but finally Ruth's doctor was reached, who

---

*Author's note: According to Maryland law, there are two definitions of death. One is brain death—complete and irreversible loss of all brain and brain stem activity. The other is cardiac death—when the heart stops. See Organ Donor Instructions for pertinent information.

phoned to assure me she would see that everything was handled promptly and correctly. Though a bit complicated in the doing, I found this experience a heartwarming one in terms of the caring and competence shown by all of the Johns Hopkins people.

# Sudden Death

There is no way to prepare for a sudden death of a loved one except to practice a mindfulness of death—to make death so much a part of your being that you are ready at any given moment to let go. There is shock, yes. There is grief. There is time that hangs heavy and still and air that gets sucked away. Walls freeze, houses cannot breathe, and the breath is caught on the intake in a silent scream. There is all of that and, with mindfulness, there is also a healing into a deeper place.

When you awaken to your own mortality, life becomes more precious, relationships are more meaningful, and regrets are minimized and reconciled. We are prepared at any given moment to let go of attachments, even to each other. Even with the shock of a sudden death, deep down we know that eventually grace seeps in like the steady drip from a lifesaving IV tube. And with that grace we are opened up to knowing that our loved ones are not lost to us, but are even more accessible to us in their transformed state. We can now be with them at any time and have our say. When they die, we expand and we become infused with their energy and their wisdom. When he needs greater security, my son says, Mom, you will never die. And I say yes, I will, and you will go on and when you die, I will go on, and I share with him all the thoughts I have written here. I have had these conversations frequently with all of my children. They know, even as they look to me as their anchor, that inside each of them is the grace of knowing the impermanence of life. This knowing allows us to love each other best.

Continue to practice befriending this presence of death that walks with you, and know that even after a knockout punch you can still rise from the canvas. Please read Ken's story . . .

> *Farewell! God knows when we shall meet again.*
> *I have a faint cold fear thrills through my veins,*
> *That almost freezes up the heat of life.*
>
> Romeo and Juliet
> William Shakespeare
> (1564–1616)

# Ken's Story

I was talking to a counselor recently about commitment, motivation, and the effects that our experiences can have on our life as we go forward. Without resolving the impact of significant events in our lives, we can find ourselves going about our daily routines carrying the burden of our emotional battering that can handicap our actions, attitudes, feelings, and, ultimately, our happiness.

On November 9, 1988, such an event occurred in my life that left me with an altered realization of life, loss, fear, and commitment. My wife of just four years, whom I adored with all my heart, was killed suddenly at the age of 26, in an automobile accident on her way to work that morning. I have searched to find a way to express the experience that results from such a life-altering occurrence. I turned to my fascination with the sport of boxing to describe the resulting struggles that I experienced.

If I look at life as if it were a boxing match, I see the excitement that the beginning of the match brings—excitement about the opportunity that being there brings, hopeful that you will do well, determined to do your best and end up a winner, and prepared to go the distance and work your way through the struggles that will occur round after round. You feel all this with the strength of body and spirit that comes from not having taken your first blow in the match.

As the match progresses, you get in some good shots that make you feel as if you are in control of the fight. Your confidence builds, and you begin to see that you can achieve the things you want to achieve. You take a few shots, but that's okay, you think, no harm done. You still feel good, and taking a few shots in the fight is to be expected. In fact you convince yourself that it is good for you—it builds character to have a little struggle on your way to victory.

Then, if you are unfortunate enough to have your guard down, and just the right moment comes along, you experience one of the most devastating events in boxing. *A "clean" right hand directly on the chin that came out of nowhere.* The short-term effect is overwhelming! Stunned, you feel your legs buckle and you lose a sense of where you are. Your senses dim. You don't even notice that you are falling over or feel any pain when you hit the canvas. You lie there for a few seconds trying to comprehend what has just happened, with no sense of what your goals or objective for the match were when you started. Then, almost out of instinct, you try to get up and get back in the match. Panic begins to set in as the rest of your body does not respond to your will to move on. You flap around on the canvas, desperate to get control of yourself and prove to yourself and those around you that you are able to go on.

Only with your own strength are you able to rise slowly to your feet, and when you get there the whole match has a new and frightening perspective. Your original plan of attack at winning this match is shattered, along with your confidence. All you are trying to do is clear your head, figure out your next move, and make sure you don't get hit again. The problem that this creates is that you tend to keep your gloves up to cover your now vulnerable chin, and you are very hesitant to throw a punch for fear that you might leave yourself open again.

In life, as in the match, the emotional damage done by that unexpected tragedy can throw you into a tailspin. Left unreconciled, long-term handicaps can develop as you try to proceed with your life and develop healthy, happy relationships. Fear of loss of a loved one and the loss of control over your life that is experienced after a sudden death can create the "gloves up" syndrome that limits your ability to open yourself up to commitment, security, and, ultimately, happiness. Only when you let go of those fears can you move on.

❧

# Suicide

In the book, *Tuesdays with Morrie*, Morrie says, "Death ends a life, not a relationship." Death by suicide, however, seems to tear at the fabric of relationships. It corrupts. It skews the balance of the survivors' psyches into a foreverness of ambiguity. It is hardly ever without blame, without shame, and without a deep and abiding regret on the part of the survivors. We do not know about the regret of the person who commits the act. Please know that we are not talking about physician-assisted suicide, which is being debated vigorously in our culture. That issue ultimately will be decided by consensus.

I have had the experience of cleaning up after two suicides, and supporting my son through a death-by-suicide of a friend. Having attended to the consequences firsthand, I would ask that if you are contemplating suicide as a "last right," that you consider the next moment. It is in the next moment that everything changes. The next moment might allow for help in the reduction of pain, both physical and mental: A veil can lift, a tear can fall, a heart can melt, a wound can heal, and hope can be restored.

Please read Alice's story, which follows and if, after reading it, you still feel hopelessly anguished, *talk to someone*! Included in the bibliography are some readings and resources that might prove helpful.

> One doth but breakfast here, another dines,
> he that liveth longest doth but sup; we must
> all go to bed in another world.
>
> Bishop Joseph Henshaw
> (1603–1679)

# Alice's Story

It was February 26, 1987 on Interstate 95, and I was heading south toward work in Adelphi, Maryland. For many years, the way to get there was to bear left, then follow the road around to an entrance to US 1. There were signs for miles warning that construction was going on and to expect lane changes. Of the four lanes of traffic, I was in the second from the right. On my right was a fully loaded gasoline tanker, and on my left was a fully loaded semi. I had been in front of and visible to both the semi driver and the tanker driver for miles, but then cars began moving into my lane to take the exit I was taking, and I slowed down until I was sandwiched between the two trucks.

The semi driver decided to move to the right then. I was about half a car length in front of him, so I did not see his turn signal blinking. I noticed the motion in my peripheral vision, though. Half my car was next to him. I sent up a prayer, "God, don't let me hit the tanker!" I could never slow down enough in time, could not move right or left, so I gunned it. And I almost made it. The semi clipped my car next to the driver's side rear tire.

This action spun my car forward and turned it ninety degrees, driver side on to the semi. I actually glanced up at the semi driver before the truck slammed into my car. Both driver's side tires shredded immediately, *but the frame of the car held.* The window next to my face never shattered, which I had expected. Because of physics and moving objects and stuff, the semi slowed down, and my car appeared to me to fly off the front of the semi. My car was rammed a total of four times, and it finally flew across the inside (far left) lane of traffic (which was *empty*) and into the median.

Somewhere during the second or third ramming, I separated into body and spirit. The body was having itself a full-panic fit, and the spirit was calm and interested in all that was happening. When I say "spirit," there are a number of words that might be used equally well. *Chi*, holy spirit, holy ghost, angel are some. I never floated above myself. The spirit stayed within the body, but separate from it. I have never felt so completely peaceful and full of love. There are no words to express that peace and love, except the ones from the New Testament: "the peace that passes all understanding." Having been there, I long to return, although a yearning is more what I feel.

When my car flew into the median, my spirit realized it was suddenly in a very light place. No tunnel, just warm, glowing light. There were beings of light there, and I know where the images of angels come from. They did not have human form, but rather were beings of pure energy that manifested itself to me as light. One being walked up to me. He was male, and very powerful. He was not Jesus. He spoke to me, not in words, but in the mind, and said, "You must go now and live." Then I was back in my car, totally stunned, body and spirit rejoined. Nothing is ever as over as a near-death experience. One instant, I was in the light, the next I was back on Earth. And all I was left with was the yearning.

You see, I had my suicide all planned. My life as an abused wife seemed impossible, and I thought I was not able to take it anymore after spending twenty-two years in mental torture. I was going to pick a really rainy day and drive my car into a bridge abutment. I wanted it to be an accident, so no one would feel guilt for it. My mother had committed suicide, so I know firsthand what survivors feel.

The being knew that, and told me I had to stay on Earth and live. That was all part of the "go now and live" communication. I cannot express how deeply and fully the message got through, but no suicide was part of it. I remember being *very* angry about that, because my one way out had been taken away.

Today, that experience has gifted me. So, too, have drugs (legal ones, that is). Without both, I could not be now fighting cancer. One sustains the body, the other the spirit. Drugs are the weapons humans use to combat microscopic life determined to rid the planet of us. It is humbling to realize that the microscopic life inside my body has run mindlessly amok. If it wins, I die and it dies with me. Does that make any sense at all?

For those trying to make sense of it all, and to find a blueprint for their lives and travails, I ask only that they take note of mindless trouble and all the havoc it wreaks in people's lives. Bad things happen to both good and bad people. And we cannot say, "Good, he deserved that," about someone we consider bad without also saying the same thing about the truly good people we know.

I don't think I deserved to get cancer. It is just part of being human. God does not cause these things to happen. They just happen. God doesn't find me a parking space close to the mall entrance, nor does God cause wars. God is in it with us, just as hurt as we are by whatever we must endure.

I see God in the strength to endure being human. I see God in prayer. I see God in community. I see God in my dog and in my son. I am afraid that a constant struggling to make sense of it all only keeps

people's minds and spirits busy with side issues and away from the
eternal grace and peace God gives us just for the taking. We don't even
have to ask for it to be there! It just *is*.

Now I know what might come next. I yearn to feel the light and
the peace that comes with it. No human words can convey the beauty of
it all. So, because I know what comes after this life, I long/yearn to be
there. I will stay here, however, because I have been given no option. You
have no idea how powerful *that* instruction is. It's just when things are
particularly rough that the longing begins to pull me. I want to go. But
I'm not a suicide. Do you get the difference? I'm completely at peace
with death. When my time comes, I'm rarin' to go.

Enjoy being physically present to each other, please. And hug each
other twice—once for me and once for you.

## Sibling Education

It's an easy thing to be a brother:
Simply fall into the world
three or four years after there's been another.
And to be a sister isn't hard:
Just sit and wait until someone
drops a loud, squirming thing in your yard.
But to be a good one, to do it best,
take that loud, squirming thing
and treat him as a guest.
And show him things he might not know:
How to make your voice light and quick
while you live deep and low;
How to cup your hands around a friend, or even make one;
How to make your face a china cup
that tilts to drink in everyone;
How to make of your eye a convex glass
that burns hot on the sweet
and lets the sour pass;
How to smile other smiles than the others do;
How to see your shell fritter and thin
while the inside part is young and new;
How to take the loud, squirming things of your own,
gather them up in the crook of your arm
till you've squeezed all the blood out of your bone.
Then, after all this, remind your brother of what everyone knows:
That there are holes out there in the yard;
That the purest thing is the one that goes.

—John F. Keener

For Cindy Keener Luzier, who was,
among many other things, a sister and a
mother, and who was never aware that
she was also a teacher.

# preplanning: now to do a really hard thing

Upon my buried body lie
lightly, gentle earth.

this is from a play co-written by
Francis Beaumont (1584–1616)
and John Fletcher (1579–1625)

When death happens the most important and immediate decision is what to do with the body. Without your say, this decision is left to your survivors, and it's always hard.

But a really hard thing is to choose in advance how to dispose of your own body because to do that means to acknowledge your own mortality, doesn't it? There it is . . . the finish line! So we put it off, hoping to put off death, but really just putting it off on someone else.

My mother, a very intelligent lady, still says, "Just throw me in the street, I don't care!" And I say back to Mom, "How many bodies have you seen lying on the street in Ridgefield, Connecticut? C'mon!!!"

Yes, c'mon! Let's do this together, for Mom and for me, because when it comes to body disposition or burial options, it really doesn't matter what you choose, just that you choose. Some of us will be bound by our own personal and cultural dictates, but whatever you choose, whether simple or elaborate, you can rest assured knowing that no one was burdened or victimized and that you took responsibility for your own departure. It's called preplanning and the choices are all yours.

# Body Donation—
# The Simplest Approach

Donating your body to a medical school for research and study represents the simplest form of disposition. In its simplicity lies an exceptional gift of parting because when we choose this type of disposition, we are choosing a benefit for generations to come.

This kind of donation, called an *anatomical gift*, goes to medical and dental schools. The Anatomical Gift Act allows anyone eighteen years or older to donate his or her body in such a way. Generally, arrangements for whole body donation must be made in advance of the expected death. You may do this through your state's Anatomy Board or directly to a medical school by writing or calling for the necessary forms. Even with prior arrangements, you should let your family, your doctor, and your healthcare advocate know of your wishes.

When donating directly to a medical school, you may be liable for the cost of disposition. Check with the institution you are considering for the specifics. However, there is usually no cost attached when donating through your state's Anatomy Board. Upon death, notification is made to the Board by the nursing home, hospital, or doctor in attendance. If there is no attending physician, the local police department should be contacted immediately. The body usually is held for two years for educational study programs at medical institutions, after which it is cremated. The family may request that the cremains (cremated remains) be returned to them, or they are buried in the state's burial grounds at no cost. Some places, however, do not return the cremains.

Remember, because the body is taken away immediately by the Board, a funeral service or wake with the body present is not possible. However, you may elect to have a memorial service at any time.

*Destiny is not a matter of chance,*
*it is a matter of choice;*
*it is not a thing to be waited for;*
*it is a thing to be achieved.*

William Jennings Bryan
(1860–1925)

# Harsh Truths Erupt Even in Sacred Places

Three giant corporations have been buying up your options in funeral services and burial properties. They have moved steadily and aggressively, gobbling up neighborhood funeral homes and cemeteries across the country. These entities usually keep the names of the original owners, leaving the community unaware of the transfer. But internally everything changes, with layers and layers of management stretching far afield of your community now pulling the strings. Where chains thrive, lower prices usually result. However, in the funeral trade, this might not always be the consequence.

The final disposition of our bodies requires choices that allow us affordability, dignity, and sacredness. As more and more independents fall to corporate takeovers, the affordability choice may become less and less, and dignity and sacredness are compromised.

It is hard to lose someone, hard to die, harder still to fear death. We don't want to talk about hard things. Continue to use this guide to help you face a hard thing and then examine your options. Like any other service provider, we need to choose the one that fills our needs and our family's circumstances.

Remember, when death happens, families usually do not shop around. In this time of personal crisis, families may be exploited, not only by the funeral trade, but by their own raw emotions—when nothing becomes too good for the person who has died. It is only through preplanning that we are assured of our personal choices, and our families are comforted knowing that they have followed our wishes.

# From Coffins to Caskets

(When dollars multiply)

Am I the greater part body
        or soul?
What is the cost of preserving a dead body
        longer than life?
Who benefits?
Is it comforting to know this dead
        body lies locked away on a sumptuous
        bed of pleated and fluted linens,
Or to know this soul alive
        dwells in you?
If they guarantee this casket, this vault,
        hermetically sealed, will keep
        me from the elements,
Will I care?
And who will check to make sure
It is so?
        Is concrete biodegradable?
        Is metal?
How large can the walled cities of dead bodies
        beneath the earth grow?
Or
Can I be buried in willow baskets
        and simple boxes
That I might feed the earth that fed me
And melt into the oneness
        of being
      me
        alive
          in you!

# the role of
# the clergy

To give light to them that sit in darkness
and in the shadow of death,
to guide our feet into the way of peace.

Luke 1:79
(KJV)

*M*any people, whether they are active in a certain church or not, will find help by calling a pastor. The moment of death is both a wrenching and powerfully spiritual event, so that having the pastor at the bedside with scriptural words of assurance may mark it as an important memory. The family may prefer to be alone at the time, in which case a pastor could provide the text of a farewell prayer and appropriate Bible passages for the family's use.

Most members of the clergy of the major religious denominations have special training in grief counseling, and in assisting families through difficult decisions both before and after a family member dies. To give spiritual assistance while considering such matters as living wills, organ donation, or withholding of life support, such a person may be the objective voice in a circle of emotional stress. Occasionally peacemaking within a conflicted extended family can be another valuable contribution. Also, in planning funeral and memorial services, and deciding between burial and cremation, a pastor's counsel can be helpful.

With the assistance of the hospital chaplain or management, hospice personnel, or a family member or friend, those who are not affiliated with a church usually will find clergy willing to come when called. If in no other way, their presence may assuage the loneliness of that time. In addition, a relationship may be introduced at this time that will continue with assistance and caring throughout the prolonged

grief process. Some churches give special training and accreditation to
laypeople whose special calling is to fulfill these kinds of pastoral
functions. The added presence of a representative of a compassionate
community can be stabilizing and much needed.

It is within all of us, however, regardless of our specialized training,
to learn how to minister to each other in times of crisis. Before we were
doctors, or nurses, or orderlies, we were daughters and sons and part of
the greater family of human beings.

> *Let brotherly love continue. Be not*
> *forgetful to entertain strangers: for thereby*
> *some have entertained angels unawares.*
>                     Hebrews 13:1–2
>                     (KJV)

A pastor friend of mine was in a large hospital recuperating from
open heart surgery. His wife Connie, also a pastor, had dropped in at
dinnertime for a few minutes with her husband. While they were
talking, a loud commotion seemed to explode in a nearby room. A man
was screaming at the top of his lungs, and embarrassed hospital
personnel were unable to quiet him. Connie, who had pastoral
chaplaincy standing in the hospital, hesitantly ventured into the hall to
see if she could be of help.

A forty-year-old son had come to visit his seventy-seven-year-old
father, who was also recovering from heart surgery. They had been
sitting together, the father on the recliner and the son in the other chair.
The father reached out to hand his son an article and, grabbing his
chest, slumped back, dead in his recliner. Medical personnel arrived
quickly, but did no more than pronounce the father dead. The scene,
then, as Pastor Connie arrived, was a young man in shock, and two
doctors, two nurses, and an orderly standing by not knowing what to
do and so remaining silent.

Pastor Connie immediately stepped in and took charge. She
directed the staff to move the dead man to the bed, clean him up, and
keep him there until the son had time alone with him. Then she took

the grieving son, who was alone in the city for his father's surgery, into a smaller room and talked with him about death as pastors do at such times. Coincidentally, her own father had died only a few weeks before, so they had much to share in a mutual flood of tears and assurances. The son was so embarrassed at how he reacted immediately following his father's death, that he wasn't sure he could walk back out to face the hospital staff. Assured that this was an understandable response, the son then asked Pastor Connie to contact his father's pastor, who, also coincidentally, was a neighbor of hers. She also knew the local mortuary to contact, and how to set about notifying the rest of the out-of-state family.

An important experience in the grief process occurred a little later when the pastor accompanied the son into the hospital room to say goodbye to his father. The pastor asked the distraught man to share what it was that he wanted to remember about his father. Looking into the father's calm, yet warm face, the tearful son shared how much his father meant to him, how devastated he felt with him gone, yet he realized his father was now where he so often had said he wanted to be, with his deceased wife.

The son said that he never thought his father would die from this surgical procedure, because he was generally so healthy and he played tennis three times a week. Even though the son had shared in the initial meeting with the pastor that he wasn't much of a believer (yes, he was raised in the church), when the pastor anointed the father's forehead with the sign of the cross, she asked the son if he wanted to pray. His immediate answer was: "Yes, please."

In the tearful prayer and packing up of the father's belongings that followed, the son began to realize that there were caring people surrounding him as he waited for his father's pastor to arrive. Before he left, the son was greatly calmed, informed about the next steps, and spiritually prepared for the pilgrimage that would lead to closure.

Later questioning of the nurses and one doctor revealed that, in their training, there was no time given to ways to assist families. The doctor said that once he pronounced death, all of his responsibilities ceased, and that it was a case for the coroner and the social services department.

# The Services of the Funeral Home

This area is often overlooked when we think about preplanning. The services of a funeral home are many, and you have the right to select only those that you require. This can be done preneed (before your death) by meeting with the funeral director and discussing the kind of service and burial option you have chosen.

It is always important (as with other key advisors) that you establish a relationship before a pressing need occurs. This is also true of the cemetery director if you choose interment (in the ground) or entombment (aboveground) burials, or choose the cemetery's scattering garden for your ashes.

Call ahead for an appointment and a tour of the facility. Conversation with the staff will give you a feel for how things will go for your family after your death. After introducing yourself and your needs to the funeral director, you should leave with relevant information and a general price list of goods and services for your perusal, along with methods of payment if you choose to pay in advance.

Unless you have an established relationship with a particular facility, you also may want to check out other funeral homes in your area. An important question to ask is, who owns the establishment and for how long? With corporate takeovers, the person you are talking with might not be there for you in the not too distant future. Independents or locally owned establishments are usually family owned and passed on to the next generation. Prices tend to be lower and services more personalized.

Having established your measure of comfort, the next step is to look at the services. All funeral homes have a Basic Services fee that is added to the total cost of the funeral arrangements you select. It includes, but is not limited to, staff to respond to initial requests for service; arrangement conference with family or responsible party; coordination with cemetery, crematory, or other parties involved with the final disposition of the deceased; preparation and filing of necessary notices, permits, and authorizations; temporary (one day or less) shelter of remains; and a proportionate share of the overhead costs. This fee also might be included in the charges for direct burials, direct cremations, and forwarding and receiving remains. This should run about $675. However, I've seen quotes of more than $3,000 for the same service.

The next major service is preparation of the body. Here it is important to note that embalming (something we all take for granted) is not required by law. The funeral home, however, may require embalming if you select a funeral with viewing or if there is long distance transporting of the body. It is not a factor in direct burial or direct cremation. Standard fee for embalming is about $300, but, again, I have been quoted as much as $455. If you choose not to embalm, there also might be a charge of up to $75 a day to refrigerate the body.

Whether or not a viewing has been selected, it is a prerogative of yours to be with your deceased loved one while he or she is in the funeral home. You may elect to attend to his or her dressing and hair care. For me, it reinforced knowing that this person, once alive, was now gone. I have never seen and felt a dead body that looks as if it is asleep. The opportunity to be with a loved one after death made me face the reality of the death and hastened my acceptance.

The funeral home is a veritable marketplace of goods and services, and everything that is offered comes with a fee—caskets from $400 to $11,000; vaults from $400 to $12,000; and cremation containers at over $3,000. It can be a one-stop shopping extravaganza offering merchandise and services that add up quickly—all the more reason for you to shop judiciously at a noncrisis time.

The funeral director must be attentive to the primary needs of your family—to your rituals, customs, religious beliefs, financial resources, and family structure—and most attentive to the children present and their needs.

When presented in a noncrisis environment, funeral home services are easy to understand and provide a good starting point for choosing a particular burial option. Making these choices before the need occurs lifts a burden from our survivors and settles the matter of final disposition of our bodies between ourselves and the funeral home.

*And with the morn those Angel faces smile,*
*Which I have loved long since, and lost awhile.*

John Henry Cardinal Newman
(1801–1890)

# Jack's Story

It was a quiet evening in the hospital, and I had hopes of going home early. I had completed my rounds as a lay chaplain and was in the office finishing up paperwork when a woman rushed in and told me an infant had just died suddenly and unexpectedly. She said the parents wanted the baby baptized by their church. That was the start of a long, agonizing, and gut-wrenching evening.

Fortunately, I was able to reach the parents' church, and the minister who was scheduled to baptize the baby in a few weeks was on call. The minister came to the hospital immediately. As I sat with the minister, I was aware of the tremendous compassion, warmth, and caring that radiated from her; she was a true blessing for the family and everyone present. I was impressed that two hospital staff members from two different departments, scheduled to leave hours earlier, stayed with the family the entire evening. The medical examiner and police were extremely supportive and sensitive to the situation and gave the family the time and space they needed.

The baptism took place in the hospital chapel. The baby was wrapped in a beautiful blanket and brought to the parents so they could hold her. As I knelt next to the minister, holding the chalice of blessed water used for the baptism, I was aware that as a clergy and a woman she was able to reach a part of the parents' heart and grief that otherwise would have been lost. And as I assisted her with the baptism and touched the baby's head, I knew I was touching one of God's little angels. The baby was beautiful and looked as if she were sleeping, but everyone in the room knew the baby would never awaken.

Although the parents were able to hold the baby for several hours to say goodbye, the moment eventually came when it was time to leave. One of the hardest and saddest things I have ever done was to walk the parents out of the hospital with only the blanket in their hands, having to leave their little baby behind.

As the days passed, I was aware I had bottled up my emotions regarding this experience. I knew I needed a way to release them and bring closure to this painful experience, so I went to the funeral. As the minister, with tears running down her face and with a choked voice, said the final blessing over the tiny coffin, "Into your hands, dear Lord, we commend the spirit of this child," I was able to let my tears flow. I am aware that my sorrow will only last a few days, but the parents' sorrow will last a lifetime.

# The Services of a Cemetery or Memorial Park

## TRADITIONAL GROUND BURIAL

If you choose ground burial, you will need to purchase:

> a casket or coffin to hold your body,
> a burial space or plot,
> a vault or outer burial container for the casket, and
> a memorial or grave marker.

To conserve space, most cemeteries are designed with double- and triple-level grave sites. Therefore, purchasing one double-tiered ground burial space entitles you to two burial rights, and, if triple-tiered, to three burial rights.

Most cemeteries also require vaults or outer burial containers. Outer burial containers are not required by state law, but their use is at the discretion of each cemetery. With heavy machinery now used for most grave digging, the vault serves to stabilize the ground above to retard sinking of the earth. Both caskets and vaults come in a wide variety, from simple boxes to fine woods, from concrete liners to space-age materials, and with as wide a spread of prices. This is an area where choosing for yourself helps your survivors greatly, because when death happens, nothing becomes too good for the one we have just lost, and we are more prone to overspend. Vaults can be purchased through the funeral home or cemetery.

The next item you need is a grave marker or memorial. The more modern memorial parks require that they be flush to the ground, which makes it easier to mow the grass and, in an egalitarian sense, allows a uniformity among persons buried there. Some cemeteries offer sections using flush markers and traditional erect tombstones. With preplanning, you also can predesign this item. Cemeteries usually require that markers be purchased through them, however, so check whether you can use outside vendors. Often, you lose your guarantee of replacement if you use an outside vendor.

Typically, a cemetery package includes the space, vault, and memorial. Caskets usually are purchased through the funeral home; however, you sometimes can use outside vendors for merchandise regardless of the funeral home or cemetery you choose. Average cost for space, vault, and memorial can be between $4,000 and $6,000. These costs may run considerably less when using church-affiliated cemeteries.

Churches and synagogues may have their own cemeteries designated for members' burials, or they may arrange with private cemeteries for an area designated for the members of that particular congregation, usually at substantially lower prices or percentage discounts.

Where in previous years, families invested in burial plots, today the entire cemetery package can be preplanned and prefunded. You may walk the cemetery grounds with a prearrangement counselor and choose your site or sites from an existing area, or save additional money by choosing in a preconstructed area. This means that the area that you buy has not been developed yet, and cemeteries offer a reduced rate for purchasing there sight unseen. Each space is then completed by adding a vault and memorial. Your memorial usually has restrictions as to size and configuration, depending on the cemetery chosen, but within these criteria, you may also predesign or even preinstall where you have bought into an already developed area of the cemetery. The only information then missing from your marker is your date of death.

Other charges associated with ground burial include fees for vault installation; opening and closing the grave site, which also entails providing a canopy, chairs, carpet, and the services of personnel to guide the procession to the grave site; installing the memorial; a perpetual care one-time, yearly, or monthly fee; and state taxes on the merchandise end of the total package. Ask questions about the charges for opening and closing the grave or crypt, which can exceed $1,000 in some areas.

Along with the more traditional burial, other options are available to you. It is worth educating yourself about the newest developments that not only can be costly when added together, but also confusing. One such option is mausoleum entombment.

## MAUSOLEUM ENTOMBMENT OR ABOVEGROUND BURIAL

Once a mostly Southern style of burial and the choice of wealthy families, mausoleum entombments are becoming available to everyone through community mausoleums. These are freestanding structures consisting of up to five levels with two-person-deep vaults on the front and cremation niches on the sides.

In a mausoleum the casket goes directly into the crypt or vault, so the space you buy is actually the vault itself. A single mausoleum space might cost anywhere from $3,000 to $5,500, and a tandem or two-person space runs from $6,300 to $9,300. Cremation niches range in price from $1,500 to $2,500. The outside granite or marble surface becomes your memorial or marker and is engraved with your name and dates directly into the surface, with extra cost for the engraving.

Additional costs include a casket, entombment fees (opening and closing), and perpetual care.

## LAWN CRYPTS

Lawn crypts are no different from traditional ground burial spaces except that the vaults are preinstalled, and the ground is supposed to be graded and layered with gravel and stones to allow more efficient drainage of groundwater. Cemeteries sell these as mausoleums underground offering a drier ground burial. With lawn crypts, the area is mostly barren of trees because the vaults are butted up against each other and leave little room for vegetation. These might be offered as a more affordable package for those who want ground burial; however, in actuality the cost differences are minimal.

## CREMATION AS AN ALTERNATIVE TO BURIAL

More and more people today are choosing cremation as an alternative to burials for a number of reasons. In our transient society it offers portability—ashes or cremains can travel and be dispersed elsewhere—and conserves land. With the rising cost of funerals, it also offers affordability. Today the Catholic Church and most other religions permit cremation.

Cremation is carried out through a funeral director who makes the arrangements with a crematory, or you may contact a crematory, whose staff includes a licensed funeral director. A cremation container is required that offers the minimum requirements for enclosure, such as corrugated board or fiberboard. The body is burned in the container. Here also, the pressure to up the quality of the merchandise can be applied. The container will be burned along with the body, so there is no need to purchase anything but the minimum required enclosure. To do otherwise renders more quantities of foreign ashes than human remains.

Your ashes then may be scattered or buried. Check your state's laws on scattering ashes. Cemeteries offer scattering gardens and cremation spaces, urns and vaults, and mausoleum niches. A relatively new burial option for ashes or cremains is a cremorial. This is a canister or pair of canisters that can hold one or two cremated remains underground with the canister(s) attached to the underside of a bronze memorial. If you choose to scatter the ashes elsewhere, you may purchase a memorial tree or bench with a plaque at a cemetery or public park as a remembrance.

Something else to consider: Having the ashes kept in a family member's home might create problems and place a particular burden on other family members. One person found it difficult to cross someone else's space to be with his mother who was enshrined in his father's china cabinet. It proved a psychological barrier for him. However, some people are unable to let go of the ashes and need the person near them while they grieve.

With cremation, you may elect to have a viewing. Some alternative establishments, such as Cremation and Funeral Alternatives in Baltimore, Maryland, allow a viewing without embalming whenever practical. The family may then rent a casket for the duration, which includes purchase of an interior cremation container. You also can elect to have a funeral service with the body present, often in church, before the cremation. Another alternative establishment, the Cremation

Society of Maryland, offers direct cremation for $645 with a one-time member's fee of $15. Independent of a funeral home and with a licensed funeral director, the society's fee covers transfer of the body, cremation, filing of the death certificate, and a plastic container for the cremated remains. Copies of death certificates also are provided at $6 each. You might want to check out cremation societies or memorial societies in your particular state for an alternative to the traditional establishments or names of establishments that offer competitive prices for funeral and burial options. Prices vary greatly from state to state.

Like all other options for body disposition, it is important to preplan, and most especially if you choose cremation. Since cremation is an irreversible process, sometimes even with prior arrangement all first-degree relatives must agree, and everyone responsible needs to sign the authorization forms provided by the funeral director. Maryland law, for example, specifies that cremation may not occur within twelve hours of death or until the body has been identified. Check with your funeral director regarding your state laws on cremation.

Talk about your preferences with your family so that if any of them have reservations about your choice, your reasons can be discussed and agreed on in a stress-free environment.

# More of Morris's Story

Even when cremation is chosen, dealing with the funeral home is not simple or altogether comforting. First, under Maryland law (I was assured by both the funeral director and my attorney), only the funeral home is allowed to provide death certificates, which may not be copies and must be provided in the original in as many originals as one needs for probate and other purposes. (I estimated ten copies, but managed with only seven of them. Each retirement agency for Ruth; my own pension funds, for which Ruth was primary beneficiary; my attorney with two copies, one for probate; and an insurance company all required certificates).

Second, the funeral home wanted to handle notices to the newspapers, but could do so accurately only if I wrote out all the needed information. I ended up receiving an average of four calls for amplification and clarification from three different newspapers.

Third, the funeral home offered (sold) a fancier box for the ashes than I chose, a guest book for the memorial service with printed sentiments not compatible with my religious beliefs, provision of flowers (my son Scot was providing our flowers), etc.

The funeral home personnel were kind, considerate, and unobtrusive throughout, but anyone not experienced with the mortuary profession needs to be armed psychologically to decline unwanted services that, when added up, are very expensive.

> *Faith is the substance of things hoped for,*
> *the evidence of things not seen.*
>
> Hebrews 11:1
> (KJV)

# Borrowing from Each Other's Traditions

As we enter the twenty-first century, I imagine all the world's religions melting into a global spirituality, creating an inclusiveness that renders all of us precious. I love that word, precious, because it cannot be compromised. You are either precious or you are not. Having been raised a Catholic, and for the last fifteen years having worshipped in a multifaith Christian community, I have grown deeper in my appreciation of other people's faith and have felt my own honored by them. This mutuality has allowed us the freedom to embrace the other while standing in our own faith. Without this mutuality I would no longer feel precious in their embrace.

I present Jewish and Islamic funeral customs because I believe them deeply honoring and respectful of the dead and move us deliberately into separating the living from the dead while still remembering and expressing our grief. This is true also of the Mass of Christian Burial.

The rites and rituals, prayers and sacraments convey that same honoring.

In *The Sacred Art of Dying*, Kenneth Kramer tells us, "Each of the religious traditions teaches, in one way or another, that the best way to prepare for one's own death is to anticipate the death experience while yet alive." Buddhists practice what is called "mindfulness of death."

> To develop full awareness of death, a monk is advised to be secluded and to pay attention to the words: "Death will take place, the life-force will be cut off." When a certain facility for this was attained, the monk was directed to recall death from several different points of view: as a murderer standing in front of you, as the inevitable loss of all achievements, as the weakness of the stuff of life, and as the shortness of the moment. These meditation devices are for achieving mindfulness of death in which the truth of death is brought forth in an anticipatory fashion. By contemplating each of these separately, the meditator, paradoxically, is liberated from the fear of dying by bringing death into life ahead of its time.*

It is good to acquaint yourselves with others' religious teachings, especially with regard to death. Some we might even incorporate into our own preparation and planning for death. The more we learn about how a people approach dying, the more we honor the whole of a people's life. Consequently, all of our perceived differences melt into a common journey as we travel the sacred ground from life to death to home again.

# Jewish Funeral Customs

Judaism is a faith rooted in many centuries of life, worship, and experience. Its principal teachings come from the monotheism of antiquity and continue to center in corporate belongingness and individual responsibility. There is no teaching of an afterlife, yet death is not seen

---

*Kenneth Kramer, *The Sacred Art of Dying: How the World Religions Understand Death*, New Jersey: Paulist Press, 1988.

as a finality. It is neither a punishment nor abandonment, but rather an integral part of creation; as God said to Adam and Eve: "for dust you are and to dust you shall return." Death, therefore, is both an inevitable part of life, and an intensely spiritual experience for family and friends.

Jewish funeral customs are very explicit and traditionally adhered to. They include watching over the body until burial (a service often provided by the funeral director), cleansing the body and wrapping it in a shroud (for men usually a *talit*, or prayer shawl), a funeral and graveside service where the *kaddish* (a mourner's prayer) is recited, burial within twenty-four hours or not more than three days after death, observance of a three-to-seven-day intense mourning period called Shiva, and the unveiling or dedication of the memorial within a year of the burial.

There is no viewing in Jewish tradition, and embalming is forbidden except when the body must be carried over long distances for burial, or when an early burial is delayed for any reason. The coffin is made of wood (no nails or metal handles). Metal caskets and concrete burial vaults would retard the natural processes.

The funeral service is usually held in the home of the deceased, in the funeral home chapel, a synagogue, or at the cemetery. An ordained Rabbi or an informed Jew conducts the funeral service. After prayers at the cemetery, the casket is lowered into the ground and family and friends shovel the dirt onto the casket—"ashes to ashes and dust to dust."

> *. . . No, the ache of the heart will not*
> *suddenly disappear . . .*
>
> The Jewish Way in Death and Mourning
> Maurice Lamm

# J. Mitchell's Story

The phone rang at the Rabbi's house where I was staying while my father was in the hospital, a few minutes before the Sabbath ended. The Rabbi and I knew what the call might mean. I had just left my father that afternoon, after saying my afternoon prayers at his bedside only two and a half hours earlier. My father had been in ICU for a week already. His condition had been deteriorating each day he had been there.

I burst into tears when Rabbi Jeret gave me the news from the call he had just ended. My father had died at 8:00 P.M. on the 11th of Av, 5759, July 24, 1999, just before the close of *Shabbat*. When the time to get ready to meet my father's body at the funeral home came, I was resolute, yet so unbearably sad about what I now had to do. I called my sister once the Sabbath ended. We talked about how we knew this was coming, yet the news was still crushing and heartbreaking. I told her I would make all the arrangements and meet my father's body at the funeral home. At that point, I was in a state of limbo, being an *onen*, one who is wrenched out of normal, but not yet having buried the deceased parent or sibling or spouse or child. This is a short period of time, hours only, when one is grieving, but not yet taking on the roles and responsibilities of a mourner.

We sat, the Rabbi, the funeral director, and I, and calmly discussed and decided matters of eternal importance. I had to ask myself: "*If* it matters for the sake of my father's soul, and my relationship with him for all eternity, what choices must I make *now?*" The chasm between my comfort levels and desires and what I had to do for my father stretched in front of me, and I knew that I would never have any doubts or regrets if I did it according to Jewish law.

So I saw my father for the last time, right there on the table in the funeral home on which his body would be ritually prepared (*tahara*) for burial the next day. My father, known for perpetual motion, was so incredibly still. I stroked his face and talked to him, retrieving his wedding ring from his finger in order to give it to my sister, and kissed him on the forehead in a kiss of goodbye. I left him, taking with me the unbearable pain of losing my father, yet being clear that his world was now different from mine. Now it was about the progression of his life in spirit, with me, his only son, as one of his important worldly anchors.

I sensed a great turmoil in him in the next world as I spoke to him of the reality he now faced. I promised to do what I could to honor and tend him from this side: to say the *Kaddish* prayer as is incumbent on Jewish sons, at least three times each day. *Kaddish* is not about death, or mourning or sorrow. It's only about an affirmation of our praise for and sanctification of God's name. There is power in its recitation for the spiritual progress of the deceased on the other side. It was beautiful to me that I could continue to honor my father even after his death in such a direct way.

So his body was ritually prepared: washed and shrouded by religious men who give of themselves in their devotion to tend to the dead. He was placed in a simple pine coffin, which was then watched through the night by religious men, reciting psalms. I felt such gratitude that by adhering to Jewish law so much love would be lavished on my father before he was to be buried.

One of my two sons was in Israel, so my other son and my wife had to come from Baltimore to northern New Jersey the next morning. In spite of the distance, I felt them both at my side, and my wife honored my dad and family by making arrangements for us to sit *Shiva* in New Jersey and Baltimore.

When we were at the cemetery, we tore our clothing, as is Jewish custom. The rent in the fabric we wear for the seven (*Shiva*) days from the day of burial reflects the permanent tear in the relationship with the person we bury that day. We buried my father near his father and mother and brother. The Rabbi recited a prayer in which it seemed every other word was "rock." How extraordinary, since the grave that I selected within the family plot almost couldn't be used. It was filled with an enormous boulder, left over from the last ice age. The irony was perfect, the rock being just like my father. He had worked until he was ninety, having had his best business years in his eighties. He was the unstoppable one, the durable, persistent, unalterable one. Just like a rock to be replaced by a rock! I eulogized him through sobs of tears. I became a mourner that afternoon, and as I write this I am only five days away from ending my time to be a mourner for my mother. She died twenty days after my father.

We sat *Shiva* in New Jersey with friends and relatives rallying around me, my sister, and our family. The pain of leaving there after three days when one would normally not leave the house for seven days was raw and near the surface as we traveled back to Baltimore. Normally, those first seven days provide a cushion to insulate and protect the mourner from everyday living while in the fragile state of being a new mourner. Then we began mourning in Baltimore, with mirrors covered in the Jewish tradition, with the community of friends and family coming to our home. They were so incredibly available and gracious, providing food and attending early morning and evening prayer services in our home. When the *Shiva* period ended, I got up and went to synagogue and was welcomed back into the community outside the confines of our house. That began the remainder of the thirty days of *Sheloshim*, the first thirty days after burial. During that time, one doesn't shave, cut hair, or pay undue attention to personal appearance or adornment.

Thus began the remaining ten months. The following ten months, bringing the total mourning time to eleven months is the period of the recitation of *Kaddish* for a parent. The remaining eleven months close the full year, until one's status as a mourner ends for a parent. For a sibling or spouse or child, the mourning period totals one month. Until one ceases to be a mourner, celebrations and entertainment are put aside in favor of more circumspect behavior out of respect for the dead. So, the cycles of Jewish mourning for a parent contain the period of being an *onen*, then *Shiva*, *Sheloshim*, the eleven months for *Kaddish*, and the year. How incredible to honor all of the natural cycles within a full year with the stages of grieving and mourning. All through the different parts of this past year, I felt the rightness of the slow emergence from the depths of grief and loss, to the beginnings of resuming "normal" activities, to no longer being a mourner.

As I began to settle into the routines and changes in my demeanor and behaviors after my father died, my mother died. My father died just before *Shabbos* ended, and my mother died right after *Shabbos* had begun. Three *Shabboses*, twenty days after my father had died, she died of respiratory arrest. He was ninety-two and a half and she was eighty-six and a half. The loss of both was crushing, and to this day I can't separate the feelings of losing one from losing the other. With my mom's death, the same cycle began again, yet different and mixed with mourning for my father. Now, today, since I am no longer mourning for my father, I mourn exclusively for my mother. Do I still grieve for my father? Yes. But I have not been a mourner for him for weeks. I'm now in the period of about three weeks when I'm exclusively mourning for my mother.

Am I still sad over losing my parents, whom I had for almost fifty-one years when they died? Yes. Do I love my parents boundlessly and timelessly? Yes. Do I know the customs and laws of Jewish life stayed me through the process of grieving and mourning my parents? Yes. Was I comforted at every turn in the path already laid down for me by hundreds of generations of Jewish mourners? Yes. Has the last year been an anguishing journey, which nevertheless bolstered and secured my faith? Yes and yes again!

> Is it well with the child?
> And she answered, it is well.
>
> 2 Kings 4:26
> (KJV)

# Rhona's Story

My father died last year. Although we loved each other, we seemed like oil and water. We were very adept at "pushing buttons" no matter how hard we tried to avoid it. Just prior to his illness, we had a big argument.

Consequently, at the hospital, I felt very alienated from him, which intensified the pain that much more. Because I was at a loss as to what to say as he lay there dying, I whispered the *Shema* in his ear. The *Shema* is the first prayer kids learn in Hebrew school, and is supposed to be the last thing one says on his or her deathbed. "Hear O Israel, the Lord is my God, the Lord is One."

Had I remembered, I would have blessed him. The blessing I am referring to is the one said at Bar and Bat Mitzvahs, at weddings, and on Yom Kippur. It is the priestly benediction: "May the Lord bless you, and keep you. May He make His face to shine upon you, and be gracious unto you. May the Lord turn His face unto you, and give you peace."

As my grandfather was dying, he blessed the nurse who was taking care of him. My grandfather told my father to get something to eat, and that he would bless my father later. My grandfather died while my father went to get something to eat, and my father was always heartbroken that his father never gave him his final blessing. Because of this, every Yom Kippur, the Day of Atonement, my father would ask forgiveness of each of us for any hurts he may have caused, and then he would bless us. It was always very emotional, because he would remember his father and cry while he was blessing us. Consequently, we would all cry, and then there would be lots of hugs and kisses.

I wrote this letter to my father to try to feel closer to him when he was in the hospital and could no longer communicate. All of the hurts, slings, and arrows, intended or not, from childhood to adulthood, seemed to dissipate after the composition of this letter. I never took the letter to the hospital, but I did read it at his funeral. It was a wonderful release for me, and, I believe, for him as well.

> Dear Daddy,
>
> It seems only fitting that I write to you, considering writing letters has been such an ongoing thing between the two of us. This, however, may well be the most difficult letter to date.
>
> Our relationship has been a long, fascinating, loving journey. You have taught me many things—some directly and some indirectly. You have taught me to examine myself first during times of conflict. Because of this, I usually try to think before I act, and try to anticipate the consequences of my actions. You have taught me to be kind to strangers—picking up hitch-hikers so often when I was young. Even now I pick

them up, *if* they have swollen ankles (you can't fake swollen ankles no matter what camouflage is tried). Doing for others for the pure joy of it, with no thought of repayment, was another lesson. I also learned *tzedakah* from you. I take great satisfaction in being able to support causes that I believe in. I have tried to live an honorable life—being faithful, supportive, and understanding where my family was concerned. I am proud of my efforts, proud of my perseverance in trying to preserve my family, and proud of the way I have handled myself through various difficulties. I learned this perseverance from you. We knew we mattered.

"They" say that we pick our parents and our children before we are born. I am not sure why we picked each other. I do know that I learned from you, and the experience has made me a better person. I hope to some degree that you feel the same.

I love you Daddy. I always have and I always will. Even as you lie dying and unable to communicate, I am hoping by writing this letter, we are somehow able to connect.

You will be leaving us soon. For you that is good— you will see Grandma and your Dad, Aunt Henrietta, Uncle Max and Aunt Jennie, and all of their children. You will also see a lot of your Army buddies and tell and relive your Army stories with people who can really understand. For those of us left behind, your passing will be bittersweet. We will know that you are no longer confined to a body that took you away from us long before your spirit was set free. You will be whole again, with all of the dignity, pride, and vitality for which you have been known throughout your life. But you won't be here.

We won't be able to see you, to listen to your Army stories for the umpteenth time, to have you eat off of our plates, to get that funny look on your face when you are overcome with emotion, but think that you are hiding it from us. We won't be able to hug you or be hugged by you. We won't be able to get your funny fish kisses, or hear you sing "Hanayrose" on Chanukah in your inimitable style and tune. And, we won't have you to bless us on Yom Kippur. And, oh so many things that I can't remember now, but will catch me off guard at the most unlikely times.

We will all miss you. We know that you will be with us in spirit, but obviously it will be a poor substitute. No matter where you are, no matter what form you're in, please be with us always, to guide us and to love us, and "may the Lord bless you, and keep you. May He make His face to shine upon you, and be gracious unto you. May the Lord turn His face unto you, and give you peace."

# Islamic Funeral Customs

Like the Hebrew word "Shalom," the word "Islam" means God's peace and well-being. Islam, together with Christianity and Judaism, comprise the three major monotheistic western religions. The basic creed of Islam is, "There is no God but Allah and Muhammad is his Prophet." People who practice Islam are called Muslims and gather to worship in mosques. Islamic religious practices vary in geographic locales; however, the Muslim funeral and burial rites seem to be universally observed.

When death occurs, the body is washed either by a member of the family or someone knowledgeable in that area. The body is then wrapped in a plain white cloth and transported in a plain wooden coffin to a mosque, where funeral prayers are said by an Imam, the local clergyman. Prayers are recited by those present in a standing position, as it is disallowed for Muslims to bow or prostrate themselves to anyone but Allah.

The deceased is then removed from the coffin and placed in a deep grave on their right side, facing Mecca. Mecca, the holiest city in Islam, is a city of Saudi Arabia, 500 miles south of Jerusalem.

As in Judaism, embalming is not allowed, and therefore burial must occur as soon as possible after death. Islam does allow donation of body parts, preferably Muslim to Muslim, and allows donation of certain parts to determine the cause of a death.

Muslims pray five times a day (sunrise, mid-morning, high noon, mid-afternoon and sundown) and believe in a spiritual death and rebirth. "Spiritual death," as described by Kenneth Kramer in the book, *The Sacred Art of Dying,* "refers to dying while still alive, what Hindus call *moksha,* what Buddhists call *nirvana,* what Taoists call *wu wei,* what Zen calls *satori,* what Jews call living the Torah, what Christians call *kenosis,* and what Muslims call *fana.* In each instance spiritual death is a rebirth in which fear of physical dying is overcome, in which internalized anxieties and doubts are de-repressed, in which a deathless spirit is realized."

> *Whoever likes to meet Allah,*
> *Allah likes to meet that person.*
> The Qur'an

# Lufti's Story

As a Muslim, I believe that the Qur'an is the word of God, and through that God has sent to us His message and His commands. Obeying the rules that are revealed to us through the Qur'an, Islam's holy book, is itself a virtue. Therefore, practicing the Islamic tradition is one of His requirements that I would like to fulfill.

Death is the most important issue to be considered in our life. Death has two faces: one dark and the other shining. The dark and fearful face of death, which is also the common person's approach toward it, appears when we look at it without inspiration from faith. As a Muslim, my approach is very different. Although seemingly cold and fearful, the real face of death is warm and lovely. To me death is not the end of life, but, on the contrary, is the beginning of real life. All difficulties are gone, it is the time for joyfulness. I consider death as a change of residence from one location to another, where I will reunite with thousands of friends and greats such as, Adam, Noah, Abraham, Moses, Jesus, Muhammad and all of the other prophets and saints who are considered stars among humans.

The Islamic tradition suggests that both death and life are gifts from God. Just think for one second: If there were no death, all of your ancestors would be alive now and unable to eat, drink, or even go to restrooms. All of them would need your help, and life would be extremely boring, even unbearable. Therefore, death is a bounty from God to all living creatures. If people knew its wisdom, they would not hate death, but would value it. Again, this positive perspective on death is for the faithful. As for those who don't believe in this understanding, death is a destroyer of all joyfulness and life, an unbearable burden.

When we talk about death as a family, it is with the above-mentioned understanding of death. Not afraid of it, we acknowledge our responsibility toward God and humanity by discussing death.

I am preparing for my death every day. I do so by doing good deeds, helping people, and practicing my other religious duties such as performing the five daily prayers. After carrying out all of these things, I will ask God's mercy and grace, remaining hopeful about that. Consequently, I don't trust my works to define my place in the hereafter, but I trust in my Lord's mercy and grace.

Last year, my grandfather died, and I was sorrowful at his departure. But I was also hopeful about his life in the hereafter, believing he was going to a better place. Some in the Muslim tradition report a saying: one thousand years of happiness in this world cannot be compared to one hour of life of the hereafter. Also, it is said that one thousand years of paradise cannot be compared to one hour of seeing the beauty of God. Therefore, you must be happy for someone who was well-prepared. My grandfather was a very kind man and helpful to everyone. I believe God will reward him in the best way. Thus, his death was not a destructive, but rather a telling, experience, causing me to realize death's inevitability. And, although I was sorry, I was also very hopeful. It was not an eternal separation, because I will go there too, and, surely, I will meet with him to tell him of our worldly life stories.

When I first approached Khaled and Samar, it was to learn of their Muslim practices regarding death. I was told before arriving at their home that Samar was to give birth any day with their fourth child. When I arrived on the evening of our interview, Khaled greeted me and offered an apology that Samar, given her condition, might not join us.

Soon after, however, she entered the room, warm and gracious, and we began our chat. What unfolded then touched me deeply. A story of their infant son, Karim, started to emerge and eventually crowded out other topics. I was aware that Samar needed to tell this story and also aware of her husband's protective presence. Gradually the wariness dissolved as Karim's presence filled the room and sheltered us in a unity of spirit. This is their story.

> *But now the child is dead, wherefore should I fast?*
> *Can I bring him back again? I shall go to him, but he*
> *shall not return to me.*
>                          After 2 Samuel 12:23
>                          (KJV)

## Khaled and Samar's Story

Samar—Muslim women are discouraged from attending funerals and going to the cemetery. A woman is considered too emotional, which is not believed to be respectful of the dead. When my grandfather died, my grandmother was sad. She was losing her partner of many years, and her grief was that of the custom. My mother, however, grieved differently. She cried and took her grief to the cemetery believing she was unable to survive without my father.

After Karim died, my son of eight months, I woke up one day and knew I did not lose him. This is not a loss I thought. He came; he visited; I loved him as best I could, and he moved on. He became a better person.

Khaled—I did not want to remain selfish. He was so sick, so many surgeries, ten before he was six months old, and us always hoping he would be better. At least now, he is not suffering. I did my best for eight months. He knew we loved him.

Samar—In Islam, there is a concept of heaven and hell, except for the children. Children are always angels. Now I am expecting a baby that I didn't know was to happen. Before Karim, I never thought that I could have a child that could be so sick, that could die. But my first experience of death with my grandfather, even as a young girl, made me grow up. It allowed me to take things as they happen. And still, when death happens, you worry about losses. You check on your parents. A baby, though, you take for granted. My difficulty was in trying to understand how God could send this brand new baby to me sick. Then you look around the hospital and see so many other babies, all so sick, and you stop worrying about everything.

Khaled—So many healthy children are neglected and so many mothers with sick children begging God for their health. Computers crash and you fix them. How can I fix this child? It is unbelievable how much technology there is. So many wires coming out of him. I couldn't believe it was my child. Tubes, wires, analysis. When would he be better?

Samar—As wonderful as the doctors were, this was a large teaching hospital. There was excitement, a chance to practice, to learn, to have a new experience, to use this amazing technology. When will he be better? And then, you know, doctors don't know that much.

Khaled—Tubes, ventilator, machines surround my tiny baby, and he no longer looks human. They wanted to intubate him for the rest of his life.

Samar—They wanted to tube feed him every three hours, this tiny baby who wouldn't gain weight, who couldn't tell them where it hurt, who couldn't sit up for relief when the weight of receiving nourishment lying on his back became too much. I was his mother. I had to fight for him. I said I will hold him and feed him. And if he gains weight, will you let me take him home? I was negotiating.

Khaled—They wanted to keep him on a ventilator. It was the hardest thing I have ever done but I refused. I respected his body. I believed if he had the will to sustain life, he would. If not, I needed to accept that.

Samar—They told us when the ventilator was removed, that he would die. They said within the half-hour, he would die and Karim kept breathing. After twelve hours, they said, now his brain is dead. Don't tell me this, I said, he is breathing—a miracle.

Khaled—He is kicking and pushing before lapsing into a coma, before dying peacefully in my arms.

This is not a unique story. We were learning through seeing other children, other parents, some of whom never visited, leaving their dying children to volunteers to hold. The nurses would beg for the parents to come, and they did not or could not. This is not a unique story. He was just our child, our experience. Because we had not been there before, for us, it was *the* experience. You become wise. You see how precious life is.

Death is the end of this life, and life is a process that leads to the afterlife—a test, an experience—the rewards come after death. We are Muslims. We read the Qur'an. We believe in God, in Christianity, in Jesus as healer, teacher and prophet, not as the only son of God. We believe in Judaism and all of the prophets from Abraham to Muhammad. We are called to pray, to fast, and to visit Mecca if we can.

We have seen extremes. We don't like to teach our children extremes. Islam is Islam, rules are the same, but customs are different in different areas. We have lived together in harmony with others of different faith. I went to a Catholic school and my father supported it. He believed you become wise when you learn other religions. When you learn Islam, it makes you stronger. Islam tells me to listen to my heart.

# Christian Funeral Customs

For Catholics, Christ is the center and the sacraments pre-eminent. The dying is administered the "last rites," earlier called the Sacrament of Extreme Unction. Today's term, "anointing the sick" involves placing holy oils on the eyes, ears, nostrils, lips and hands and feet of the dying, with the priestly prayer, "May the Lord who frees you from sin save you and raise you up."

Protestant traditions are widely diverse, coming from many different national and historic sources. The basic liturgical pattern for most of the older mainstream denominations is that of the Episcopal "Book of Common Prayer." The present edition, dated 1977, and in current usage, offers a simple and usable list of suggestions on pages 506, 507, applicable across all denominations, emphasizing that a Christian burial is an Easter service, celebrating the promises of the faith. Lutheran, Presbyterian, Methodist, Reformed, and United Church of Christ among many others have similar models. Some title their liturgies "Witness to the Resurrection."

On the day or evening previous to the funeral, a showing or visitation, also called a wake by Catholics, is held in church or mortuary chapel, with the casket open and relatives and friends paying respects. Since most faith communities do not object to embalming, burial can be delayed until a convenient time for mourners, especially if they are coming from a distance.

The funeral itself consists of a service of prayer, scripture readings from both Jewish and Christian scriptures, and a eulogy given by clergy or family member. For a Catholic, the Rite of Christian Burial also includes the distribution of Holy Communion. Usually held in a church or mortuary chapel, this service continues to the graveside, where a final commitment blessing is given. Sometimes the Jewish custom of throwing soil on the casket is used. ("Ashes to ashes, dust to dust.") Across the spectrum of differing histories, some churches have minimal guides for the content of the ritual, leaving the family's taste to rule. In some churches, the casket is closed before the service starts and is brought into the church by clergy and family; in others the open casket remains central. When the burial precedes, the gathering is usually called a memorial service.

As a general rule, interment or entombment is the final act, differing from the Jewish practice which may include sitting Shiva for three to seven days after the burial. There is no doctrinal opposition to cremation, or burial at sea. Many older local churches have cemeteries, but their rules for admission vary greatly. The majority of Protestant congregations today will extend clergy and public services to non-members and their families. The more conservative communions may have their own limitations on "outsiders," and need to be respected for their standards. Usually the funeral director will know the different churches' traditions and will assist families in making decisions.

In all Christian traditions, the support of community is very important. Friends can be most helpful to the family by staying in touch immediately and long after a loved one has died. This is a time when the loss is most deeply felt. Listening to and allowing the survivors to talk about the death and the deceased are important elements of the grieving process. Your presence, even in silence, provides comfort and a healing salve.

## THE FUNERAL SERVICE

There is great comfort for many in the rites and rituals that are a part of a Christian funeral ceremony. Most often in this type of service the body is present, and sometimes the casket remains open. Historically solemn and structured, funerals have begun to be personalized in recent times, to varying degrees. It is most important to talk with your religious leader about your wishes and about the elements that are important to you.

Recently, I attended a Mass of Christian Burial for a local pastor, The Reverend Monsignor Anthony L. Sauerwein of St. Louis Catholic Church in Clarksville, Maryland. The congregation and Monsignor Sauerwein were honored with the presence of His Eminence Cardinal William Keeler, Archbishop of Baltimore, who presided.

The church was filled with all levels of clergy, family and friends, past and current parishioners, flowers and incense, great hymns sung by a full choir—" Ave Maria,""How Great Thou Art,""On Eagle's Wings"—and filled with prayers, the body and blood of Christ embodied in the Communion or Holy Eucharist, and the pageantry and splendor of a high holy funeral Mass.

It was awesome, and one bowed in the face of such holiness. But it was The Most Reverend Andrew McDonald, Bishop of Little Rock, Arkansas, and Monsignor Sauerwein's best friend of sixty years, who touched us, who moved us—to laughter, to tears—who, in his homily, brought the palpable presence of his friend into that auspicious gathering by telling us that,"Before he was known as 'Monsignor Anthony Sauerwein,' God called the thirteen-year-old 'Tony.'"

And it was this intimate tapestry of a life woven tenderly and humorously—woven with the sacred stitches of a sixty-year friendship—that caused the congregation and the high clergy to erupt in spontaneous applause.

Bishop McDonald, or "Andy" as Monsignor Sauerwein knew him, provided a clearing in the rites so that we might see past the holy to the human shape. I was grateful for this touch, for the duality of sacred and secular that brought me in touch with my own holiness. Funeral services can do that.

> *We do not have to be whole to be holy.*
> *You can be a very cracked pot and be holy.*
>
> Pastoral Care Staff
> St. Thomas Hospital

## THE MEMORIAL SERVICE

The memorial service can be described as a funeral service freed up. The body usually is not present at this kind of service, which may occur days, weeks, or months after the death. In our transient society, multiple services at different locations are not unusual.

Participants share freely about the life, values, and uniqueness of the deceased, and it is not uncommon to have an open mike for spontaneous sharing. This format allows for originality, humor, and an aliveness that suggests an inclusive spirituality. It might be preplanned by the decedent or reflect strongly the deceased's spoken wishes.

Many elements can be drawn in to this type of service: songs, pictures, a video snapshot of the deceased's life, skits, paintings, and any imaginable agreed upon tribute. Within this framework, there is ample room for delightful surprises that can bring laughter and joy in the midst of great sorrow while following the rituals of a culture and a community. It is the people and the memories they share that define this kind of gathering.

## THE MEMORIAL PROGRAM OR BOOKLET

A printed memorial can be one page or several. It usually contains a biography of the deceased and the Order of the Memorial or Funeral Service. It also can include tributes to the deceased, pictures, poems, whatever you are moved to create. It can be simple text without adornments or rendered artistically.

It can be a memorable keepsake of the deceased for friends to take away from the service, and it can also be distributed or mailed to those who could not attend.

You can predesign a memorial booklet completely or choose just the photographs and the obituary. However, helping to create a memorial booklet done by friends and family is often a welcomed oasis from the shock and numbness of having you physically gone from their lives.

## LEAVING OUR MARK

We all leave our mark, our imprint, here in this world. We leave it in the hearts of those we have loved, and in the hearts of those who have loved us. We may leave it intentionally preserved in home movies, in letters, and in photo albums, and sometimes in archeological dig sites, like the attic or basement, or buried in the faded memories of aged relatives.

There is a growing realization of the importance of life histories for our families where the threads of generational intimacies can become entwined. Here in Maryland, my friends Anne and Sam have started a retirement business called, "Before I Forget: Life History Videos" that is meant to do just that. And nationally, the Association of Personal Historians (APH) is dedicated to helping people preserve their life stories and memories through writing and through audio and video means. (The association can be reached at http://www.personalhistorians.org).

Consider recording your voice and image and thoughts for your family. This enduring gift to them might make your new "home" seem not so far away.

*In my Father's house are many mansions . . .*
*I go to prepare a place for you.*

John 14:2
(KJV)

# A Father's Day Message

Dear Daddy,

Now that you're gone, and I don't have an earthly father any more, I find as I celebrate my first Father's Day without you, I want to celebrate your life as my father.

I have had so many wonderful memories of you this springtime. As I was planting some Nasturtium seeds a couple of weeks ago, I could suddenly hear your voice through the late afternoon breezes calling me, "Little Chum, come help me plant the garden." I closed my eyes, and suddenly you were there carefully showing me how to lay the seeds in the straight rows we had just made, warning me not to plant them too deep! I felt your hand over mine as you helped me carry the "it's too heavy, Daddy" water bucket to give the seeds their first drink.

There was something very worshipful about being out in the open fields with you on those sunny days. It was as if God made me just to be your daughter. You taught me to treat the earth, the trees, especially the water very carefully, as if God handed them just to me! (You always were big on turning off the water faucets so they wouldn't leak!) You said God made the water and all the plants that grew for us, as long as we cared for them and didn't waste them.

I remember carrying your four o'clock snack out to you in the field watching that I didn't let the coffee spill from your old leaky thermos—I felt like a "big girl" being entrusted with such an important job! As I now sit and read my words under the big tree that shades our home, I remember how you used to share your snack with me while I would sit inside the big hollow tree that we discovered together. Do you remember how upset Mom was the time I came home covered with lice from sitting in that old tree—she said she would probably have to cut off all my hair!

Too quickly, my eyes open as a car drives past, and I know that I am not with you on the farm after all. Funny how I can remember these things now, but I didn't while you were still with me and we could have shared them together. Please know that I will always miss you, but in the way God made this glorious universe that you taught me to love, we all have to go on when we lose a dear one.

When you were so sick, I didn't want you to feel any pain and so, as awkward as it felt, I prayed that you could feel our love and would go quickly to be with God. I wish I could have asked you if that was alright—I think you would have said "yes." I knew you believed in prayer because we always started each meal with the one your Mom taught you, "Come, Lord Jesus, be our guest, let these gifts to us be blessed." You were a man of faith and integrity. You never missed a Sunday taking us to church. Even when the crops needed harvesting or the hay had been cut down and would get rained on if it wasn't baled that very afternoon, you would not go bale it— not on Sunday! You would never violate your basic ethics and principles, even if it cost you a lower yield. I learned to put worshiping God as the highest priority of the week, because you said, "If God only worked on six days, so should we." Because of what you taught us, my brother and I have honored the importance of the spiritual. That was your standard and it became ours, too.

David and I honored your prayers, your daily devotions, your Christian convictions, and your godly life. As it is said, "Children never have been very good at listening to their parents, but they have never failed to imitate them."

You were dedicated to your family. We were always secure in the knowledge that you loved us and protected us. When you had to discipline one of us, we always knew it was in love, though we resented it. "A man prides himself on his strength," goes the old adage, "but when his child is born he discovers that strength is not enough, and that he must learn gentleness." When all of us cousins would be together for a family picnic, we would ask you to hold out your hands so we could take turns putting our hands inside of yours. You had the biggest, strongest hands any of us ever saw! Yet, you were always and foremost, a "gentle-man."

You opened the doors of the full life to us. You gave us what we needed, you stood by and let us learn some things the hard way; but you were always nearby with a word of encouragement.

Yes, you have gone to be with your parents, brothers, and sisters. However, David and I have more than memories to recall and enjoy. We have you with us, in our characters, ethics, faith, and outlook on life.

On this Father's Day we honor you and give thanks to God that we were chosen to be your children. In honoring you, we also give homage to all the fathers whose children are blessed as we are.

Your loving daughter, Corinne

⚭

# Preplanning Versus Prepaying

The argument still rages over whether prefunding or paying in advance is to your benefit. Before you do, with either a funeral home or cemetery, ask questions such as what happens if you move to another location after contracting with a local establishment, what exactly can be prefunded, where is the money held, what guarantee do you have that it is secured, is it a lump sum payment or is financing available, what are the interest rates, what are the additional costs involved at the time of death (labor costs such as opening and closing the grave and late in the day or weekend burials), and so on. Prepaying for funerals can lock in a price and is usually transferable to another state, although if the price is higher in the state you are transferring to, you might be liable for the difference. Prepaying for a funeral also can help families with limited means to qualify for medical assistance. The funeral money (up to a limit determined by each state) cannot be used for anything else, such as paying a hospital bill.

Remember that funeral homes and cemeteries by law must give you an itemized list of all of their services and merchandise and prices. The best way to shop is to call and make an appointment with each at their facility. So-called prearrangement counselors who prey on the public through telemarketing, using scare tactics and thumbscrew sales-manship, do not have your best interests at heart. Theirs is a world of high commissions and hurried training. With rare exceptions, once in your homes, they are hard to get rid of.

If you choose to preplan without prepaying, money must be set aside to cover the cost of funeral expenses through an irrevocable funeral trust. This allows for no use other than for funeral expenses. Insurance policies may not be readily accessible to cover these costs and are also meant to provide for the living. However, remember that setting aside money for funeral expenses without preplanning is not enough to unburden your loved ones. A trust or insurance policy cannot get up and go shopping. Without prior arrangements made by you, that is what your survivors will have to do when you die. The most heartening experiences I have had with families who have suffered losses is witnessing their relief and comfort at discovering that all of the myriad details they would have had to attend to were handled already by the deceased. It is truly a gift of love that will be remembered. And it is unfortunate that so many of us have to be pushed into making this gift. I pray that this guide and the stories shared on these pages will inspire you to create this most precious gift for your loved ones. Please start your research today, gather your information, make your decisions, and give yourself a deadline to complete your funeral arrangements. The Funeral Arrangements form in the Appendix can then be completed. I guarantee that, with this last piece in place, you will begin anew to live life to its fullest.

∽

*Now God be praised, I will die in peace.*
James Wolfe
(1727–1759)

# Ellen's Story*

 The image of my father lying dead on the floor of the small bathroom in his apartment is the one that is most frequently on my mind now. I come back to this fresh memory when I want to touch again—and again—the strange fact that my father has died.

The image of his body, stretched out as it was, neat and straight, even in those tight quarters, is not a frightful one for me. It reminds me of the familiar picture of Gulliver on the ground surrounded by hundreds of Lilliputians trying to immobilize the giant. I see a huge man in some fantastic situation. Dad was a man whose size and bluster made him a towering presence even in a crowd.

I wanted to write about the gifts Dad left me in his death at nearly 77 years of age. It is not the three dozen plastic containers with lids or the furniture with its authentic 50's look that I speak about. It is about

---

*"Parting Gifts" by Ellen S. Zinner (Ellen's Story) was first published in *The Forum Newsletter*, vol. 24, issue 5, September/October 1998, p. 5, by the Association for Death Education and Counseling. It is reprinted here with the association's permission.

the intended and unintended events that served my sister and me well immediately upon learning about his death.

The first of these was my phone call to Dad the evening before his death. I called him late from my office to talk about the conference that I was to attend that weekend. We discussed his chronic ailments and problems sleeping, talked of world news and March Madness basketball. When we hung up, Dad called back immediately to say that he loved me and that my sister and I were the reasons he kept going on. I told him I loved him, too. This conversation came to me in a heartbeat of being told, at the airport just before my intended departure for Chicago and the conference, that he had been found dead in his apartment.

Dad has not suffered aging lightly. He had difficulty coping with the discomforts and infirmities that his weight and years of smoking were engendering. He wasn't afraid of death, but he did fear dying alone in his apartment lest his body not be discovered for days. So, he had wisely arranged for a morning check-in service, TeleCare, and it was they who made the call to his apartment manager who ultimately found Dad within a few hours of death. It pleases me to think that this small wish of his was realized.

From the airport, I was able to locate the funeral director with whom Dad and I had met almost three years ago. Dad had seen the director's name in a local magazine article on funeral homes. This particular funeral director was spotlighted as offering the least expensive funerals in our city. Dad had never cut loose from his Depression roots. When he and I arranged his funeral, price was a major consideration. He deviated from the most frugal arrangements on only two things— having a curved-top casket and arranging for a funeral car to carry it to the cemetery. These were his luxuries. It made me smile then and now to know that he "treated" himself to a few indulgences whose price tags he thought outrageous. Of course, Dad thought the cost of milk, bread, cereal, and gasoline was outrageous!

On his death, it was a great help to my sister and me that the funeral home had been identified and Dad's preferences established. Throughout the service and burial, we knew that we were doing what he wanted. One cousin said that he half-expected Uncle Lou to sit up and applaud the show.

Dad had left all of his papers in order. You might think that perhaps he had some premonition of his death, but the truth is that

Dad's papers have been in order for the last decade. The will, original copies held by several people, was over 20 years old. Among his bankbooks, Social Security, and Medicare cards were left little notes reminding us to ask for the $200 rent deposit (with accrued interest!) that he had given 17 years before. He had cleaned cupboards over the years by giving us dishes and knick-knacks that he no longer wished to store. He had done his homework with all of his accounts so that we would not have to labor. He made it easy, and we knew it.

These are the gifts that seem apparent and important in this first week after his demise. He removed every obstacle he could, so we would be left to our own business of remembering and grieving.

# Veterans Information

When we think of service to our country, veterans hold a sacred place and are honored with special benefits for their survivors at the time of their death. There also may be other survivor benefits for your spouse and dependent children available to you.

A burial and funeral expense allowance may be paid for deceased veterans, who, at the time of death, were entitled to receive pension or compensation, or would have been entitled to receive compensation but for the receipt of military retired pay.

The plot or interment allowance is no longer payable based solely on wartime service. Eligibility is limited to the same requirements as the burial and funeral expense allowance described above (changed by the Omnibus Budget Reconciliation Act of 1990).

*Veterans benefits must be applied for; they are not paid automatically.* Claims for nonservice-connected burial allowance must be filed within two years after burial or cremation. There is no time limit for filing claims for service-connected benefits.

A free burial in a national cemetery is also available to eligible deceased veterans. The burial can be in any national cemetery that has space, except Arlington. The free burial includes opening and closing of the grave, the grave marker, and, if available, an honor guard. An American flag may be issued to drape the casket. Burials are also available to an eligible veteran's spouse and minor children. Under certain conditions an unmarried adult child can be buried in the same site.

Free burials in a national cemetery can be requested at the time of death only by contacting the director of the national cemetery desired. Several publications are available:

+ "Interments in National Cemeteries," which describes services available to veterans and dependents
+ "List of National Cemeteries," which lists the names and status of each federally owned national cemetery
+ "Application for Headstone or Marker—Department of Defense Form 1330" (the monetary allowance in lieu of a government headstone or marker has been eliminated)

These publications and other information on free burial services for veterans can be obtained by writing to the Office of Chief of Support Services, Memorial Division, Department of the Army, Washington, DC 20315.

For information on headstone and markers, call 1-800-697-6947. For other information on death benefits, call the Veterans Benefits Administration (VBA) at 1-800-827-1000, or use its Web site, www.va.gov

When filing a claim for veterans benefits, most or all of the following documents are needed:

+ veteran's death certificate
+ veteran's discharge papers
+ copy of veteran's marriage certificate
+ birth certificates of veteran's minor children
+ receipt of itemized funeral bill for veteran

The types of benefits that are available and the necessary qualifications for those benefits do change periodically, so it is important to obtain up-to-date information. You can contact your local or regional office of the U.S. Department of Veteran's Affairs for current information on benefits and claims procedures, call the Department of Veteran's Affairs, 1-800-827-1000, or write Department of Veteran's Affairs, 810 Vermont Avenue, N.W., Washington, DC 20420.

## ARLINGTON NATIONAL CEMETERY

Although space is limited, and burial at Arlington National Cemetery is restricted to only a few categories of those who have served honorably in the armed forces, retirees are among those eligible for Arlington burial. They include: "Those having at least 20 years active duty or active reserve service which qualified them for retired pay either upon retirement or at age 60, and those retired for disability."

Other categories of those eligible for burial at Arlington include those who have died on active duty; veterans honorably discharged for 30 percent (or more) disability before October 1, 1949; holders of the nation's highest military decorations (Medal of Honor, Distinguished Service Cross, Air Force Cross or Navy Cross, Distinguished Service Medal, and Silver Star) or the Purple Heart; certain POWs who died on or after November 30, 1993; the spouse or unmarried minor (under age twenty-one) child of any of the previous categories or of any person already buried in Arlington; an unmarried dependent student up to age twenty-three; an unmarried adult child with physical or mental disability acquired before age twenty-one. (Note: The previous categories are described only generally. For detailed information or evaluation of particular cases, contact The Superintendent, Arlington National Cemetery, Attention: ANNC-ADI, Arlington, VA 22211, or call 1-703-695-3250.)

In addition to ground burial, Arlington has a columbarium for cremated remains. Any honorably discharged veteran, that veteran's spouse, or his or her dependent children may be inurned there. The ashes of a person who meets the criteria for burial can either be inurned in the columbarium or given ground interment, according to the wishes of those eligible or next of kin. Contact the above address or phone number for information about shipment of cremated remains.

*When you loved me I gave you the whole sun and stars
to play with. I gave you eternity in a single moment,
strength of the mountains in one clasp of your arms, and
the volume of all the seas in one impulse of your soul.*

George Bernard Shaw
(1856–1950)

# Carole's Story

The last words my mother said to me were, "I don't want to leave you." She knew she was important in our lives and it was hard for her to imagine her children's lives without her in it. She had a miserable last marriage and because of that and her health problems, she relied on us, my brother and myself, heavily. She knew she was pretty demanding.

Between her marital troubles and her illnesses, I thought to myself, I don't ever want to do this to my children. She occupied my day off every Wednesday. Mother's needs came before my husband's and my children's. She just never had a sense of anyone else's time. One day, I remember, I arrived at her house early in the morning and did not leave until late in the evening. She bid me farewell by saying, "Thanks for dropping by."

I never thought about how much I gave. I just did it. I remember one day my son said to me, "Mom, your life will be so much easier when you don't have all of this responsibility." And I felt so hurt! I couldn't believe that he would think that about Gammy even as I can now appreciate what caused him to say it.

Part of me thought then, "How could he think that my life will be better without her?"

She took a lot but she also gave. She allowed us in to pray with her. We expressed ourselves to her and she accepted our expression. We formed a little circle of love around her and wrapped her up in prayers. She was non-religious but we sensed that our prayers gave her a feeling of peacefulness.

Towards the end our rabbi came to the house to lend support. He spent the day watching us as we went through the hospice procedures and when I thought I could not go on, he sat with me and held my hand and very softly and lovingly said, "Carole, ask God for strength." He helped me to feel the experience and surrender to it, and I began to feel stronger. My brother and I became even closer and formed an even stronger bond in this time with our mother.

After she died I wanted so much to speak at her service. I went in the study and closed my eyes and asked God to help me to get up. It wasn't original and I was scared and nervous, but I got up and said this prayer of remembrance in a strong voice that surprised me and my children:

> In the rising of the sun and in its going down,
>    we remember them.
>
> In the blowing of the wind and in the chill of winter,
>    we remember them.
>
> In the opening buds and in the rebirth of spring,
>    we remember them.
>
> In the blueness of the sky and in the warmth of summer,
>    we remember them.
>
> In the rustling of leaves and in the beauty of autumn,
>    we remember them.
>
> In the beginning of the year and when it ends,
>    we remember them.
>
> When we are weary and in need of strength,
>    we remember them.
>
> When we are lost and sick at heart,
>    we remember them.
>
> When we have joys we yearn to share,
>    we remember them.
>
> So long as we live, they too shall live,
>    for they are now a part of us,
>       as we remember them.

# Social Security Information

Social Security provides benefits not only when you are alive, but also to your survivors after your death. In addition to your spouse, or ex-spouses, if you were married for at least ten years, eligibility may extend to your dependent children and dependent parents. Previously, you had to request this information in writing from the Social Security Administration. However, a new law, passed in 1999, allows you to receive this information yearly, about ninety days before your birth month, that estimates the retirement, disability, and survivor benefits you are eligible to receive now and in the future. It is important that you keep up-to-date on what those benefits are for your family. These statements are sent to those Americans who are age twenty-five or older. When you receive your annual statement, go over it carefully. Check the information against your pay stubs, W-2 forms, and tax returns to make sure all earnings are correct. Make sure each year you have worked is included. If you discover an error or need information prior to receiving your statement, call the Social Security Administration, 1-800-772-1213.

Even though the cost of funerals continues to rise, the benefit for burial allotted through Social Security remains at $255. This and all other benefits, based on income, *must be applied for; they are not paid automatically*, and they must be applied for within a certain time.

You need most or all of the following when filing a claim:

- death certificate
- birth certificate of deceased
- Social Security card of deceased
- marriage certificate
- birth certificate of applicant
- original divorce decree certificate
- birth certificates of minor children
- disability proof for children over age eighteen
- itemized funeral receipt

*There are no graves here.*
*These mountains and plains are a cradle and*
*a stepping stone.*
*Whenever you pass by the field where you have*
*laid your ancestors, look well thereupon,*
*and you shall see yourselves and your*
*children dancing hand in hand.*
*Verily you often make merry without knowing.*

*The Prophet*
Kahlil Gibran
(1883–1931)

# About Life

Memorial benches, stones, and trees mark the almost three-mile pathway around Lake Centennial. It is where I go each morning to walk, to keep my heart pumping, to breathe in and out. I am alive and breathing! I walk briskly, now passing a bench affixed with a small brass plaque that reads, "In Loving Memory of our Friend and Colleague Paul Kerschner."

I do not stop, but the name resonates softly in me and I, not knowing, muse about Paul's life and his energy, now released into the air that I am breathing, now a part of the gravitational force that keeps me grounded. The air around me becomes energized, and I am aware as I breathe that I am connected to all of creation, to all that was and is and will be. It is the same with each memorial for each person that I pass, and I am grateful to the families and friends who have allowed me to share in the celebration of all whom they have loved, in this public place.

# The Importance of Community

Some people become so integrated into your life that they almost seem a part of you, and you are always comforted by their existence. They are there to be accessed with a spoken word or as an automatic response to life's vicissitudes. For me those people are my family and my community, the latter being wrapped around the former. Family includes my nuclear and extended family, and community comprises all of my special interest groups. Together they are friends who form my support system and the infrastructure of my being. That one of my special interest groups is my "faith" community seals my foundation.

My faith community is the largest entity outside of my family that can be accessed and set in motion with a single phone call or, nowadays, a single e-mail. It is programmed to respond in its entirety when one of its members is hurting, threatened, celebrating, or dying. Responsiveness can take the form of prayers, phone calls, letters, cards, e-mail, visits, meals, parties, and healing or celebration services. Often, the difference between being a part of a larger community and not might be the difference between loneliness and a sense of belonging.

When I returned home after my father's death, I was greeted with many cards of condolence, phone calls and hugs, and willing ears, and was given a unique opportunity to share from the podium during a worship service how my father's death affected me. My experience contrasted greatly with that of my brother, who felt very much alone with his grief. It seems that after being with his immediate family, he still needed consolation from a wider audience. Community provides this consolation, and a "faith" community provides ongoing consolation.

This ongoing consolation in community can be dispersed among many people with each person offering his or her individual expertise from that person's own comfort level. For some, preparing meals might be more comfortable, for others, a degree of separation via e-mail is more acceptable. My friend, John, who has terminal cancer, accesses me for death talk. Every few weeks, my phone rings and it is John greeting me with, "Hello, Deathlady, let's have lunch." Our time together then is spent talking about his fears, about his dying, laughing out loud to release the pressure, maybe taking in a movie afterward, and always ending tenderly with hugs and I love yous. I know when I don't hear from John that he is busy focusing on life and pushing away his dying. I am glad to be used in this way, even when he tells me fondly: "You do know you're weird, don't you? You do know that you're not normal?" By that he means that very few of us are able to go to those places, to the place where he is going. I am privileged to walk with him. This is community.

A community can be made up of those of the same faith or it can be multidenominational or nondenominational. It can be a group of people who share the same interests and activities, as in a tennis community, meditation groups, writing groups, discussion groups, or the like. Inherent in community is fellowship or companionship—a mutual sharing. A truly supportive community, however, is one that knows its members and allows each his or her own uniqueness. A community of close friends is an added bonus.

Why am I sharing this with you? Because a new acquaintance recently confided in me her need to reach out and find a support outside of her family. She realized that her small family, aging and dying, could no longer support her. She was casting around now for a community that could "hold" her as her family continued to decrease in numbers. She wondered if I had addressed the issue of community in this book. I said yes, but to my surprise I realized that my internal yes would not serve her as she needed. I had become so accustomed to having a sense of belonging that I did not feel the need to write about it. It seemed inherently contained in most of what I already had written. Her yearning, however, stirred in me a need to examine more closely that sense of belonging and caused these pages to be written. I hope they prove helpful.

*In the dark womb where I began*
*My mother's life made me a man.*
*Through all the months of human birth*
*Her beauty fed my common earth*
*I cannot see, nor breathe, nor stir,*
*But through the death of some of her.*

John Masefield
(1878–1967)

# Bill's Story

When my mother lay dying, I told her she'd been a good mother. And at one point I heard my own voice say out of the silence, "I've been a good son!" Like we're closing the books now, not going to carry anything forward.

What's helped me in grieving my mother's death has been the support of friends and family. Cards, letters, phone calls. One good friend wrote, "We have become the old ones now." That was oddly comforting because my friend named what I was feeling.

The first fifty days I was incredibly busy, making arrangements, sorting through keepsakes. I ran from my grief. But these last seventy days I've allowed space for tears. I've given in to the silence. Solitude has brought good grief. I'm especially aware of my mother in late afternoons. It was usually then I'd call her. And the tears come . . .

⊱⊰

*Where is the Life we have lost in living?*
*Where is the wisdom we have lost in knowledge?*
*Where is the knowledge we have lost in information?*

T. S. Eliot
(1888–1965)

# Jo's Story

I am a part of her. It was within her womb that I was protected and nourished. We shared that precious time together . . . all our own.

Together, my mother and I struggled to give me life so that I might touch, see, smell, taste, hear, and grow. You see, in the beginning when I was conceived, the plan was that Mom and I would have years and years together, to laugh at silly things, to spend hours chatting about nothing of importance, to cook together, shop together, and whisper about my first boyfriend.

My mother was supposed to be here for me. She was supposed to comfort me and provide me with unconditional love, but something went haywire. So, I have spent a lifetime missing her, a lady that my mind will not allow me to recall.

They tried to keep her from me, my Dad and all the other grown-ups in the family. They thought that if I didn't talk about her, if I didn't see pictures, if I wasn't allowed to ask questions, that I would forget. They thought that I was brave, that I had adjusted to her loss. They said that I was "a real little trouper." What they failed to realize was that my very existence was all the proof that I needed that Mom was once very much in my world.

I had my own secret way back then when I went into my room feeling very sad and all alone—Mom was right there with me. And as I peered into the mirror at my image, trying to figure out who I was, I could only see a part of me. The smudges that were all too apparent served only as a reminder that underneath it was me, there was her, there was my Mom.

I used to think that there would come a time, when I was all grown up, that I would no longer need Mom in my life; that I would no longer feel the ache caused by her absence, but I was wrong. What I have come to recognize is that with no loving memories of my mother to hold onto, I can't seem to fill the void that remains within my soul.

# epilogue

## 11

The rest of the story . . .

*B*efore the shock of his death dissolved, Carol was already experiencing Paul's tender touch. She first discovered it among his papers in the multiple obituaries that he had written, along with instructions as to where to place each: a gift to ease the process.

Carol said she fell in love with him all over again in the way he left personal records, diaries, and journals. It was so easy, she said, following in his footsteps preparing necessary information for eventual tax reporting. The documents and figures were all there, neat and tidy, another gift.

Paul's life as a writer (he was cited in the *Guinness Book of World Records* as the most prolific comic book writer of all times), and as a collector of Latin American art, took him to colorful places. To recompose Paul's life and his varied journeys would have been an enormous task for Carol.

He left no distractions to her grieving, which, over the months following his death, poured out of her, in memories, in tears, in the radiant fold of his love, and in the way she shared all of that with us.

Months later, stripping a room of its flowery wallpaper and repainting with a sky blue background more appropriate for hanging the comic art collection, she discovered on the back of one Lone Ranger piece, in Paul's own handwriting, written two years before he died, "For my kemo sabe Carol from her deceased spouse, Love, Paul."

Paul left a true legacy of love—his gift to celebrate life. And it goes on . . .

# ten truths about grief

It was just a little point of light, this life we harbored, just a
tiny beam of consciousness, frail beyond measure, brief and
unsustainable, the greatest lives like the smallest ones, delicately
held together by the merest thread of breath.

*The Chatham School Affair*
**Thomas Cook**

1. It is global, numbing in its enormity, hardly able to be
   contained.
2. It is personal, chewing on the heart, a painful, gnawing
   presence.
3. A lot of people are afraid of it, of experiencing it, and watching
   it.
4. A lot of people are in awe of it.
5. We move in awe and fear around it, praying that you survive,
   admonishing you to survive, helping you to survive,
   knowing/not knowing if we could survive.
6. No one is immune to grieving—not kids, not animals, not
   anyone.
7. There are no rules or time frames for grief.
8. Grieving brings us to a deeper place.
9. People who grieve into healing are our heroes.
10. Grieving is living and forgiving.

෴

*She went her unremembering way,*
    *She went and left in me*
*The pang of all the partings gone,*
    *And partings yet to be.*

*She left me marvelling why my soul*
    *Was sad that she was glad;*
*At all the sadness in the sweet,*
    *The sweetness in the sad.*

Francis Thompson
(1859–1907)

# Miriam's Miss Nell

Miss Nell's snoring no longer disturbs me. At first it would pull me awake, but now it evokes a settling in the deepest part of my soul where Miriam lives. The last time I saw Miriam, Miss Nell's owner, she was snoring deeply in a room rich with woody grains, a room that held you in its bosom and made you feel a slow, old-fashioned kind of lazy comfort. A soft hum in the background of movement and the wheels of care turning, then tender hands administering, and a lilting voice inquiring, "Are you family?"

"No," I replied, "a friend," as I helped her turn Miriam ever so gently. When I first walked in and said her name, she opened her eyes, looked at me, and said my name. Then she slipped back into the deepest slumber that made me appreciate how far she had traveled to acknowledge my presence. This was the Hospice Center where Miriam sleeps. Until I touched her and mentioned Nell. Then she became active, every muscle activated to respond, eager to settle this matter. So I patted her softly and whispered in her ear, "Relax Miriam and know that Nell will be fine. We'll take good care of her." With that she settled back into a snoring slumber.

I didn't really know Nell, but knew of her. Knew that she was Miriam's beloved pet, a four-year-old shar-pei, Miriam's only child, whom she took everywhere, especially for long rides in her open air

Volkswagen Cabriolet that she stuffed four of us in last summer at the beach and tootled down the ocean highway while we sang at the top of our lungs. That weekend, she was experiencing a chronic pain down her legs, complaining that it had started with a tennis lesson without proper warm-up stretches a few months earlier. I took her out on the courts later and, after extensive stretching, played instructively with her. She wasn't complaining then.

She did complain, however, and was extremely uncomfortable when sitting on the enclosed porch of the beach house with five of us—including Miriam—talking about death and the book I was writing. I read excerpts at intervals and listened as each piece evoked a response. One woman, another guest, poked her head in, quickly scoped out the topic, and deemed it not appetizing for early morning. She retreated promptly. The conversation continued for another hour, and Miriam was not happy. Twice, she stood to leave and each time, with great effort, relented.

What she wanted to tell me was this. How she was with her father at his dying. And then she said, promise me that when you write this book, with everyone's notion now of how to do it right, that you not make me feel wrong because I did the best I could. And I promised her that.

A few months later, and after she had attended my wedding looking radiant, she was lying in the Hospice Center with cancer eating away her bones and Miss Nell on her mind.

The call from Peggy, her friend dating back to kindergarten, came two weeks after Miriam had died. Peggy said that her work schedule at the hospital had increased and that she was unable to keep Miss Nell, that it was unfair to have her alone so much, that she prayed and prayed on it and that my name kept coming up in her prayers. Would I consider taking her?

My husband and I considered. He of the Virgoan sign of the stars, linear, logical, a harms/benefit kind of guy trying to communicate with me, the Saggitarian, my stars strewn all over the place in exquisite creative chaotic order. But he persists, all the while knowing he's going down under the weight of Divine Providence that points us toward Nell and a new blended family.

Peggy introduced her to me as "Miss" Nell, the princess. And I introduced her to Dennis as such. He rolled his eyes. In a flash she was in our bed snuggled between us with sadness pulled tightly around her. Nell was grieving.

Nell was grieving. And she took her grief and bolted out the door trying with all her might to outrun it. I took out right after her. Hours later she had clashed with three dogs. I tried running ahead of her, flagging the owners of other dogs on leashes to protect their pets. I shouted at them as I ran, about her loss, about her pain, and gained their sympathies along the way for the most part. When Dennis finally brought the car to us and coaxed her in, she was bleeding from a head wound that required stitches and ended up with a shunt in her neck from a puncture wound. Shaved and stitched and wounded beyond measure, we brought her home, heavily sedated, where she behaved for the duration of her convalescence. I talked extensively to Miriam then about anger.

The next time she bolted, she took me on a merry chase, testing my endurance, but always keeping me in sight. Exhausted, I retreated to home after delivering her to Miriam's divine guidance. This time she returned and sat in front of the house just out of reach while I talked to her about trust. She didn't seem angry then as she slowly wrestled with whether she would allow me to love her . . . and allow herself to love again.

It's been over six months, and Miss Nell has found a home in our hearts and in the hearts of her extended family, our grown children. Her separation anxiety grows less and less. If we travel, she goes to my daughter's house, where she is entertained by three cats and fussed over by my son-in-law who alternately calls her Nelvis, or Nelvina, or Nelbert. My out-of-town daughter, when she visits, takes her jogging. Miss Nell comes to the office with me each day and is greeted happily by our staff. My grown-up son tortures her with hands-on love/play, and Dennis pipes in when Nell's story is told, that maybe the "praying" that Peggy did was of the "preying" on our emotions kind. We ignore him.

When we returned recently from a vacation, after nine days of being away from her, she greeted me on two hind legs with the other two circled around my waist, and her wrinkled face yearning earnestly as if to say, "Mom, I thought you were never coming back!" I melt.

Note to Miriam: "You did it just right! Goodnight, sweetheart."

# grieving is living

In this sad world of ours, sorrow comes to all, and it often comes with bitter agony. Perfect relief is not possible, except with time. You cannot now believe that you will ever feel better. But this is not true. You are sure to be happy again. Knowing this, truly believing it, will make you less miserable now. I have had enough experience to make this statement.

Abraham Lincoln
(1809–1865)

When we experience death, our grief is not an interruption of life. Our grief is part of life. We are meant to be present to our grief and to those around us who grieve.

All day long my enemies taunt me . . . They bring in meals—casseroles of ashes!

*The Message*
*New Testament with Psalms and Proverbs*
Eugene H. Peterson

There are seasons of the soul when life hands us "casseroles of ashes." When death happens, we get the taste of ashes in our mouth. We are tempted to rush past our grief; we don't want to taste our casseroles of ashes.

I will give you the treasures of darkness . . .

*Isaiah 45:3*
(KJV)

---

"Grieving Is Living" was written and shared by The Reverend William F. Hug, Ph.D., after the death of his mother. Grief counseling is available through hospice and other agencies. Grief groups can be a wonderful support because you are with people who understand what you are going through and can share your pain.

Ours is a God who says, "Stick with your casseroles of ashes, and I'll give you the treasures of darkness." Sometimes it is only in the valley of the shadow of death that we get to know God in the deepest parts of ourselves. Sometimes it is only in the valley of the shadow of death that we get to know who our true friends are. The treasures of darkness can only come to us when we tolerate the darkness!

Wynton Marsalis talking to David Frost about jazz said, "It's not how you play a note, but how you move from note to note. There's juice in that silence between notes. You want to dip down and get some of that juice. That's what's healing!"

What a wonderful thing to say! You want to savor that juice in your hurting places. Your healing is in those silent grieving places. We are meant to savor our grief in the same way Wynton Marsalis savors the silence between notes.

What about you? How do you cope with death? Who in your life lets you be sad when you need to? Lets you be confused, angry? And who tells you, "Get on with your life," because they want you to feel better so they'll feel better. When you connect with a grieving person you feel powerless. You feel what they feel and that is good.

And how are you and God talking about grief these days? Have you gotten angry at God lately? Sometimes that's the only way through. To tell God how angry you are that this person you loved has died, has left you. Before we can get to the sweet promises of Psalm 23, we have to pass through Psalm 22 with its haunting, "My God, my God, why hast thou forsaken me?"

Ours is a God who meets us where we feel we've lost our best friend in this life. Ours is a God who invites us to stay with the grief until God can show us the treasures of darkness.

So stop rushing from note to note. Let there be room for silence. Dip down into the rich juices of healing for which you yearn. Grieving is living. Do it well! Eat your casseroles of ashes and let God show you the treasures of darkness.

And through it all remember those good words of Julian of Norwich—that wonderful saint from the fourteenth and fifteenth centuries, the first woman to write a book in English:

. . . all shall be well,
and all shall be well,
and all manner of thing shall be well.

# a eulogy for sammy

From Journal to my In Utero Grandchild
2/27/00

*When a child is born, the entire universe has to shift and make room.*

*Spiritual Midwifery*
Ina Gaskin

Sweetheart—

If you could have seen your parents today—how they
held each other, how tenderly they spoke to each
other, how they cried together in such a heartfelt
way—as they grieved the death of their beloved cat,
Sammy.

Sammy was loved by both, but he was your mother's
baby before you. He was picked by her, the runt of
the litter, scrawny with ear mites and worms. They
brought him home and nursed him to robust
health—the kind of nursing that only full hearts can
do—and Sammy thrived, full of mischief and play
and a full-blown exuberance for life. Maybe he knew
that his life would be short, so he packed it with as
much glee as his heart could hold.

While he delighted with his antics, he brought with
him gifts to bestow. For Kayha, their very mature
matriarchal feline who was wounded by mistreatment

and also rescued by your Mom and Dad, he brought healing. Cautious and wary as she was of risking play or people's intentions, he showed her the joy of play and daring to let herself trust. She allowed him his presumptuousness with an air of mock intolerance that gradually grew to a noticeable fondness. Now Kayha, too, is grieving at his sudden absence from her life.

For your Mom, he brought a very special gift. For you see, it was Sammy who made her believe that she could be a mom—and she was everything a mom should be to him. Waiting for you to be born, she dreamt of nursing you, with Sammy lying on her lap and Kayha nearby. She dreamt of having all of her "babies" to hold. And when he took his last breath in her arms, her cry was for the shock of his sudden death, for losing him, and for all the future moments with him now lost to her. Your Dad, hearing her cry, matched her agony of shock and grief.

They wrapped him tenderly in a towel and laid him in a basket. The next morning they buried him in the cats' graveyard in your paternal grandparents' yard and placed an array of daisies over his small grave. I left them tonight, still holding each other and crying and sharing stories—delightful stories—of Sammy's days and nights with them.

Sammy came into this world undersized, but with a heart big enough to hold life. And he lived it full-out—never holding back. I was privileged to be with your Mom and Dad as they remembered him with gratitude for what he had brought to their lives. It was one of the finest memorials I have witnessed—to sit with your parents and honor a cat's life—Sammy's life—now crossed over the Rainbow Bridge, waiting, waiting . . .

Perhaps he passed by you on his journey there. Did you smile at each other?

A Eulogy for Sammy is dedicated to
my first grandchild, Elena Satenig Johnston,
born May 29 in the year 2000.
With love,
Gammy

# appendix: questionnaires and forms

In this section are questionnaires and forms that enable you to provide, all in one place, the information your family or friends will need in case of your disability or death. It may take some time to gather this information, but it will help immensely the people you are depending on to help you on your journey home. As you work your way through this task, if it seems too big a burden, know that it would be an even bigger burden for those you leave behind. For a sense of accomplishment, check these items off as you complete them.

## Checklist of Questionnaires and Forms

- ❏ My Personal Information
- ❏ My Medical History
- ❏ My Family

### IF I BECOME INCAPACITATED

- ❏ Advance Directives (Living Will, Healthcare Agent)
- ❏ Durable Power of Attorney
- ❏ Long Term Healthcare Insurance

## UPON MY DEATH

❏     To Those First on the Scene

❏     Persons to Be Notified

❏     Key Advisors and Institutions to Be Contacted

❏     My Funeral Arrangement Choices

❏     My Funeral Home Services

❏     Things to Be Canceled

❏     My Last Will and Testament


## ASSET INFORMATION

❏     Life Insurance Policies

❏     Bank Accounts/Safe Deposit Boxes

❏     Brokerage Accounts and Other Investments

❏     Tangible Personal Property Inventory

❏     Disbursement of Special Items

❏     Living Trust(s)


## THINGS I MAY NOT HAVE TOLD YOU YET

❏     Statement of Wishes

❏     Special Messages to Those I Love


## LAST MINUTE CHANGES

❏     Special Instructions and Information
       (updated periodically)

# My Personal Information

Name _____

Address _____

City, State _____ Zip _____ Phone _____

Date of Birth _____ Place of Birth _____

Social Security Number _____

Military Service Number _____

Branch of Military _____

Date of Entry _____ Date of Separation _____

Military Grade, Rank, or Rating _____

Wars/Conflicts Served _____

Decorations Received _____

Education _____

Degree(s) _____

Religious Affiliation _____

❑ Single          ❑ Married          ❑ Widowed

❑ Divorced        ❑ Partnered

Occupation (or retired from) _____

Employer _____

Type of Business _____ Phone _____

Health Insurance Provider _____

Plan # _____

Father's Name _____

Address _____

City, State _____ Zip _____ Phone _____

Date of Birth _____ Place of Birth _____

Mother's Maiden Name _____

Address _____

City, State _____ Zip _____ Phone _____

Date of Birth _____ Place of Birth _____

# My Medical History

This information is important to your family now and after your death. In addition, keep a current copy of your medical records accessible to them.

I have had medical treatment for:

| | CURRENT | PAST | NEVER |
|---|---|---|---|
| Cancer | ❏ | ❏ | ❏ |
| Tuberculosis | ❏ | ❏ | ❏ |
| Kidney Disorder | ❏ | ❏ | ❏ |
| Diabetes | ❏ | ❏ | ❏ |
| Circulatory | ❏ | ❏ | ❏ |
| Heart | ❏ | ❏ | ❏ |
| Other _____ | ❏ | ❏ | ❏ |
| Other _____ | ❏ | ❏ | ❏ |

I am allergic to the following drugs:

1. _____  2. _____

3. _____  4. _____

Physician: _____  Telephone: _____

Physician: _____  Telephone: _____

Physician: _____  Telephone: _____

Medical Plan: _____  Telephone: _____

Plan #: _____  History #: _____

Dentist: _____  Telephone: _____


Other Important Health Information:

_____

_____

_____

_____

_____

_____

_____

_____

_____

_____

_____

# My Family

## MY SPOUSE/PARTNER

Spouse/Partner (Circle one) _____

SS# _____ Phone _____

Address _____

Date of Birth _____ Place of Birth _____

Spouse/Partner Employer _____

Phone _____


## MY CHILDREN, STEPCHILDREN, GRANDCHILDREN

Name _____

Date of Birth _____ Relationship _____

Address _____

Phone _____


Name _____

Date of Birth _____ Relationship _____

Address _____

Phone _____

Name _____

Date of Birth _____ Relationship _____

Address _____

Phone _____


Name _____

Date of Birth _____ Relationship _____

Address _____

Phone _____


## MY SIBLINGS

Name _____

Date of Birth _____ Relationship _____

Address _____

Phone _____


Name _____

Date of Birth _____ Relationship _____

Address _____

Phone _____

Name _____

Date of Birth _____ Relationship _____

Address _____

Phone _____


Name _____

Date of Birth _____ Relationship _____

Address _____

Phone _____

# If I Become Incapacitated

You need the following three documents in the event of your incapacitation:

+   **A Living Will** to determine life support decisions when you can't do it yourself.
+   **A Durable Power of Attorney for Healthcare** to determine who makes your healthcare decisions when you can't do that yourself. (These two items are often combined in a single document called *Advance Directives*.)
+   **A Durable Power of Attorney** to delegate authority to handle your affairs.

## ADVANCE DIRECTIVES

# Living Will and Appointment of Healthcare Agent for

_____

(your name)

(Cross through any items in the form that you do not want to apply.)

I, _____

(name)

residing at _____

(address)

_____

(city, state, zip)

appoint the following individual as my agent to make healthcare decisions for me:

_____

(name)

_____

(address)

_____

(city, state, zip, phone)

Optional: If this agent is unavailable or is unable or unwilling to act as my agent, then I appoint the following person to act in this capacity:

_____

(name)

_____

(address)

_____

(city, state, zip, phone)

I hereby grant my agent full power and authority to make healthcare decisions on my behalf, including, but not limited to, the following:

(1) To request, review, and receive any information, verbal or written, regarding my physical or mental health, including, but not limited to, medical and hospital records, and to consent to the disclosure of this information;

(2) To employ and/or discharge my healthcare providers;

(3) To consent to and authorize my admission to and discharge from a hospital or related institution;

(4) To give consent for, or to withhold consent for, x-rays, anesthesia, medication, surgery, and other diagnostic and treatment procedures prescribed or ordered by or under the direction of a licensed physician, dentist, or podiatrist;

(5) To consent to the provision, withholding, and withdrawal of life-sustaining procedures, in accordance with, but not limited to my instructions as set below;

   a. If my death from a terminal condition is imminent and even if life-sustaining procedures are used and there is no reasonable expectation of my recovery, I direct that my life not be extended by life-sustaining procedures, including the administration of nutrition and hydration.

b. If I am in a persistent vegetative state, that is, if I am not conscious and am not aware of my environment nor able to interact with others, and there is no reasonable expectation of my recovery, I direct that my life not be extended by life-sustaining procedures, including the administration of nutrition and hydration artificially.

c. If I have an end-stage condition, that is, a condition caused by injury, disease, or illness, as a result of which I have suffered severe and permanent deterioration indicated by incompetency and complete physical dependency and for which, to a reasonable degree of medical certainty, treatment of the irreversible condition would be medically ineffective, I direct that my life not be extended by life-sustaining procedures, including the administration of nutrition and hydration artificially.

d. I direct that if I am brain dead, an anatomical gift be offered on my behalf to a patient in need of an organ or tissue transplant. If a transplant occurs, I want artificial heart/lung support devices to be continued on my behalf only until organ or tissue suitability of the patient is confirmed and organ tissue recovery has taken place.

(6) To take lawful actions that may be necessary to carry out these decisions, including the granting of releases of liability to medical providers.

If it becomes necessary for a court to appoint a guardian of my person, I nominate my agent or successor agent to be the guardian of my person.

This Appointment of Healthcare Agent shall become effective when my attending physician and a second physician certify in writing that I am incapable of making an informed decision regarding my health, pursuant to any law of any jurisdiction which now or hereafter authorizes advance directives for healthcare decisions.

The authority of my agent is subject to the following provisions and limitations:

_____

_____

_____

If I am pregnant, my agent shall follow these specific instruction:

_____

_____

_____

My agent is to make healthcare decisions for me based on the healthcare instructions I give in this document and on my wishes as otherwise known to my agent. If my wishes are unknown or unclear, my agent is to make healthcare decisions for me in accordance with my best interests, to be determined by my agent after considering the benefits, burdens, and risks that might result from a given treatment or course of treatment, or from the withholding or withdrawal of a treatment or course of treatment.

My agent shall not be liable for the costs of care based solely on this authorization. By signing below, I indicate that I am emotionally and mentally competent to make this appointment of a healthcare agent and that I understand its purpose and effect.

_____          _____
(Signature of Declarant)                      (Date)

The declarant signed or acknowledged signing this appointment of a healthcare agent in my presence and, based upon my personal observation, appears to be a competent individual.

_____     _____
(Signature of Witness)                              (Date)

_____     _____


_____     _____

SAMPLE DURABLE POWER
OF ATTORNEY

# Durable Power of Attorney

I, _____ ,

of _____ (city, state),

a resident of _____ County,

hereby appoint my _____ (relationship)

_____ ,

of _____ (city, state),

Social Security Number: _____ , my

Attorney-in-Fact and s/he is referred to as my "Attorney-in-Fact" in

this document.

In the event that _____ , for any reason is

unable, unwilling, or fails to act or continue to act as my Attorney-

in-Fact, I constitute my _____ (relationship)

_____ ,

of _____ (city, state),

Social Security Number: _____ , to act

as my Attorney-in-Fact and s/he shall be referred to as my "Attorney-in-Fact" in this document.

I intend to create a Durable Power of Attorney pursuant to applicable Estates and Trusts Article(s) of my state of residence. This Power of Attorney becomes effective upon the disability of the principal.

My Attorney-in-Fact shall use the following form when signing on my behalf pursuant to this Power: "Name of Party by Name of Attorney, his/her Attorney-in-Fact."

My Attorney-in-Fact is authorized:

1.   To collect and receive any money and assets to which I may be entitled; to deposit cash and checks in any of my accounts, to endorse for deposit, transfer, or collection, in my name and for my account, any checks payable to my order; and to draw and sign checks for me and in my name, including any accounts opened by my said Attorney-in-Fact in my name at any bank or banks, loan accounts, savings society, money market funds, or elsewhere, and to receive and apply the proceeds of such checks as my Attorney-in-Fact deems best;

and to close accounts. This power includes, but is not limited to, my

account or accounts at _____ Bank,

specifically, Account Number _____; and

my account at _____ Bank,

_____, specifically, Account

Number: _____.

2.    To take all lawful steps to recover, collect, and receive any amounts

of money now or hereafter owing or payable to me; and to compromise

and execute releases or other sufficient discharges for them.

3.    To make loans, secured or unsecured, in such amounts, upon

such terms, with or without interest and to such firms, corporations,

and persons as shall be appropriate.

4.    To institute, prosecute, defend, compromise, or otherwise

dispose of and to appear for me in any proceedings at law or in

enquiry or otherwise before any tribunal for the enforcement or for

the defense of any claim, either alone or in conjunction with other

persons, relating to me or to any property of mine or any other persons, and to obtain, discharge, and substitute counsel and authorize appearance of such counsel to be entered for me in any such action or proceeding; and to enter into agreements or compromise or arbitrate any claim in which I may be in any manner interested and for that purpose to enter into agreements or compromise or arbitrate, or arbitrate and perform or enforce any award entered in arbitration.

5.  To lease, sublet, let, sell, transfer, release, hire professional managers, convey, and/or mortgage any real property owned by me, including my residence at _____

_____, or in which I have an interest upon such terms and conditions and under such covenants as my said Attorney-in-Fact shall think fit, including the sale of my real estate and to sign, seal, execute, and deliver deeds and convey- ances therefor, including the right to describe such real estate by appropriate metes and bounds.

6.  To purchase or otherwise acquire any interest in and possession of real property and to accept all deeds for such property on my

behalf; and to manage, repair, improve, maintain, restore, build, or develop any real property in which I now have or may have an interest.

7.    To execute, deliver, and acknowledge deeds, deeds of trust, covenants, indentures, agreements, mortgages, hypothecations, bills of lading, bills, bonds, notes, receipts, evidences of debts, releases, and satisfactions of mortgage, judgment, ground rents, and other debts, in relation to my residence at _____ _____, and any other property that I have an interest in.

8.    To collect on, compromise, endorse, borrow against, hypothecate, release, and recover any promissory note receivable, whether secured or unsecured, and any related deed of trust.

9.    To buy, purchase, sell, repair, alter, manage, and dispose of personal property at private sale or public sale of every kind and nature, and to sign, seal, execute, and deliver assignments and bills of sale therefor.

10. To enter my safe deposit boxes and to open new safe deposit boxes; and to add to and to remove any of the contents of any such safe deposit boxes; and to close out any of the boxes.

11. To borrow money from my account on whatever terms and conditions may be deemed advisable, including the right to borrow money on any insurance policies issued on my life for any purpose without any obligation on the part of such insurance company to determine the purpose for such loan or application of the proceeds, and to pledge, assign, and deliver the policy or policies as security.

12. To apply for and receive any government, insurance, and retirement benefits to which I may be entitled and to exercise any right to elect benefits or payment options; to terminate, to change beneficiaries or ownership, to assign rights, to borrow or receive cash value in return for the surrender of any or all rights I may have in life insurance policies or benefits, annuity policies, plans or benefits, mutual funds and other dividend investment plans and retirement, profit-sharing and employee welfare plans and benefits without any obligation on their part to determine the purpose of such requests.

13.  To take custody of my stocks, bonds, and other investments of

all kinds, to give orders for the sale, surrender, or exchange of any

such investment, and to receive the proceeds thereof; to sign and

deliver assignments, stock and bond powers, and other documents

required for any such sale, assignment, surrender, or exchange; to give

orders for the purchase of stocks, bonds, and other investments of

any kind and to settle for same; to give instructions as to the regis-

tration thereof and the mailing of dividends and interest therefrom;

and to clip and deposit coupons attached to any coupon bonds,

whether now owned by me or hereafter acquired. This power

includes, but is not limited to, my account(s), with ⸻⸻

⸻⸻⸻⸻, specifically, Account Number

⸻⸻⸻⸻ .


14.  To purchase for me United States of America Treasury Bonds of

the kinds which are redeemable at par in payment of federal estate

taxes, to borrow money and obtain credit in my name from any source

for such purpose, to make, execute, endorse, and deliver promissory

notes, bills of exchange, drafts, agreements or other obligations for such bonds and, as security therefor, to pledge, mortgage, and assign any stocks, bonds, securities, insurance values, and other properties, real or personal, in which I may have an interest and to arrange for the safekeeping and custody of any such Treasury Bonds.

15. To open or maintain accounts with stockbrokers (on cash or on margin); to buy, sell, endorse, transfer, hypothecate, and borrow against any shares of stocks, bonds, or other securities.

16. To vote in person or by proxy at all meetings of shareholders, whether general, regular, or special, of any corporation of whose shares I am the owner, on any and all questions which may arise at or come before any such meeting, and to do each and every thing respecting such shares of stock, including the calling of meetings of directors or stockholders or making and giving consents and ratifications, and any and every other act or thing which I might or could do if personally present, intending hereby to confer upon my Attorney-in-Fact full power and authority to do, with reference to such shares of stock, any and everything whatsoever which I myself might or could do as owner of such shares.

17.  To continue the operation of my business(s) belonging to me or in which I have a substantial interest for such time and in such manner as my Attorney-in-Fact may deem advisable or to sell or liquidate or incorporate any business, or interest therein, at such time and on such terms as my Attorney-in-Fact may deem advisable and in my best interests, including representing me at shareholders' meetings and voting proxies.

18.  To procure, change, carry, or cancel insurance of such kind and in such amounts as my Attorney-in-Fact deems advisable against any and all risk affecting property or persons against liability, damage, or claim of any sort, to claim any benefits or proceeds on my behalf; and to purchase medical insurance for any dependent of mine.

19.  To join with my spouse or my spouse's estate in filing income or gift tax returns for any years for which I have not filed such returns and to consent to any gifts made by my spouse as being made one-half by me for gift tax purposes, even though such action subjects my estate to additional liabilities.

20.  In Accordance with IRS Form 2848, I give my Attorney-in-Fact

_____ , of _____ ,

_____ (city, state), Social Security Number: _____ , a

resident of _____ County, or my successor Attorney-

in-Fact, _____ , of _____ ,

_____ (city, state), Social Security Number: _____ , a

resident of _____ County, the power to execute the

IRS Form 2848, Power of Attorney and Declaration of

Representative, and to prepare, sign, and file federal, state, or local,

income, gift, or other tax returns of all kinds, claims for refund,

requests for extensions of time, petitions to the Tax Court or other

courts regarding tax matters, and any and all other tax-related

documents, including, without limitation to, receipts, offers, waivers,

consents (including, but not limited to, consents and agreements

under Internal Revenue Code Section 2032A, or any successor

section thereto), Power of Attorney, closing agreements; to exercise

any elections I may have under federal, state, or local tax law; and

generally to act in my behalf in all tax matters of all kinds and for all

periods before all persons representing the Internal Revenue Service and any other taxing authority, including receipt of confidential

information and the posting of bonds.

21.  To execute a deed of trust, designating one or more persons

(including my Attorney-in-Fact) as original or successor trustee and

to transfer to the trust any or all property owned by me as my

Attorney-in-Fact may decide, provided that this income and

principal of the trust shall either be distributable to me or to the

guardian of my estate, or be applied for my benefit, and upon my

death, any remaining balance of principal or unexpended income of

the trust shall be distributed to my estate. Furthermore, the deed of

trust shall be amenable and revocable at any time and from time to

time, in whole or in part, by me or my Attorney-in-Fact.

22.  To add, at any time or times, any or all of the property owned

by me to any trust in existence for my benefit when this power was

created, provided that the income and principal of the trust shall

either be distributable to me or to the guardian of my estate or be

applied for my benefit during my lifetime and, upon my death, any remaining principal and unexpended income of the trust is directed to be distributed to my estate.

23.  To withdraw and receive the income or corpus of any trust over which I may have a right of withdrawal, and to request and receive the income or corpus of any trust with respect to which the trustee thereof has the discretionary power to make distributions to or on my behalf, and to execute a receipt and release or such similar document for the property so received.

24.  To convey or release any contingent or expectant interests in property, marital property rights, and rights of survivorship incident to joint tenancy or tenancy by entirety.

25.  To elect to take against the Will and conveyances of my spouse after death, if appropriate, and disclaim any interest in property which I am required to disclaim as a result of such election; to retain any property which I have the right to elect to retain; to file petitions pertaining to the election, including petitions to extend the time for electing and petitions for orders, decrees, and judgments; and to take

all other actions which my Attorney-in-Fact deems appropriate in order to effectuate the election.

26. To release or disclaim on my behalf any interest in property acquired by intestate, testate, or inter vivos transfer, including exercising or surrendering any right to revoke a revocable trust.

27. To renounce any fiduciary positions to which I have been or may be appointed, including but not limited to, personal representative, trustee, guardian, attorney-in-fact, and officer or director of a corporation or political or government body, to resign such positions in which capacity I am presently serving, and to settle on a receipt and release or other informal method as my Attorney-in-Fact deems advisable.

28. To have nonexclusive authority to give consent for such medical treatment to be performed on me and to authorize, arrange for, consent to, waive, and terminate any and all medical and survival procedures on my behalf, including the administration of drugs; or to withhold such consent.

29. To arrange for my entrance to and care at any hospital, nursing home, health center, convalescent home, retirement home, or similar institutions; and to pay all bills for my care as my Attorney-in-Fact, based on medical advice, has determined in good faith to be necessary and for my well-being.

30. To employ lawyers, investment counsel, accountants, physicians, dentists, and other persons to render services for or to me or my estate and to pay the usual and reasonable fees and compensation of such persons for their services.

31. If it becomes necessary for a court to appoint a guardian of my person and/or property, I nominate and consent to the appointment of my agent named herein to be the guardian of my person and/or property.

32. To appoint a successor Attorney-in-Fact if at anytime they become unwilling or unable to continue to serve as my Attorney-in-Fact.

33. To make unlimited gifts of cash and property to family, friends, or any person, including the agent, him or herself on my behalf.

I further provide as follows:

34. Except as my Attorney-in-Fact may waive same from time to time, s/he shall be compensated as such in accordance with the fee schedule of a corporate fiduciary located in my county of domicile, which fiduciary my Attorney-in-Fact may select, and which schedule would be applicable if such corporate fiduciary were serving as a trustee of my assets, and my Attorney-in-Fact may negotiate and fix the compensation of any successors my Attorney-in-Fact may appoint.

35. All acts done by my Attorney-in-Fact pursuant to this power during any period of my disability or incapacity shall have the same effect and inure to the benefit and bind me and my successors in interest as if I were competent and not disabled.

36. This power may be accepted and relied upon by anyone to whom it is presented until such person either receives written notice

of revocation by me or guardian or similar fiduciary of my estate has actual knowledge of my death.

37. All actions of my Attorney-in-Fact shall bind me and my heirs, distributees, legal representatives, successors, and assigns, and for the purpose of inducing anyone to act in accordance with the powers I have granted herein, I hereby represent, warrant, and agree that if this Power of Attorney is terminated or amended for any reason, I and my heirs, distributees, legal representatives, successors, and assigns will hold such party or parties harmless from any loss suffered or liability incurred by such party or parties while acting in accordance with this power prior to that party's receipt of written notice of any such termination or amendment.

38. I hereby revoke all prior Durable Powers of Attorney that I may have executed, and I retain the right to revoke or amend this Power of Attorney and to substitute other attorneys in place of the Attorney-in-Fact appointed herein. Amendments to shall be attached to the original of this Power of Attorney.

39. I understand that this Power of Attorney is an important legal document. Before executing this document, my attorney explained to me the following:

    (a)  This document provides my Attorney-in-Fact with broad powers to dispose, sell, convey, and encumber my real and personal property;

    (b)  This document provides my Attorney-in-Fact with limited powers concerning my health care;

    (c)  The powers granted in this Power will exist for an indefinite period of time unless I limit their duration by the terms of this power or revoke this power. These powers will continue to exist notwithstanding my subsequent disability or incapacity; and

    (d)  I have the right to revoke or terminate this power at any time.

40. Questions pertaining to the validity, construction, and powers created under this instrument shall be determined in accordance with the laws of the state of _____, my state of residence.

IN WITNESS WHEREOF, and intending to be legally bound

hereby, I have signed this Power of Attorney this _____ day

of _____, _____.
          (month)                           (year)

_____
                    (Signature of Principal)

Witness:

_____

_____

THE STATE OF _____

CITY/COUNTY OF _____

On this _____ day of _____,

_____, personally appeared before me, a Notary Public in

and for the said County and State, the above-named

_____, who acknowledged

the foregoing Power of Attorney to be his/her act and deed and

desires the same might be recorded as such according to law.

WITNESS my hand and Notarial Seal the day and year

aforesaid

_____

Notary Public, State of _____

_____

Print Name

_____

My Commission Expires

## LONG-TERM HEALTHCARE INSURANCE

I have ☐   have not ☐   purchased Long-Term Healthcare

Insurance.


The policy is located _____

_____ .

# Upon My Death

The rest of this section is devoted to providing information that your survivors may need in dealing with the affairs of your death. The urgent things are first.

## TO THOSE FIRST ON THE SCENE—INITIAL INFORMATION UPON MY DEATH

There are some things I definitely want you to do, and there are some things I definitely *don't* want you to do.

*Please do the following:*

Please don't do the following:

_____

_____

_____

_____

_____

_____

_____

_____

_____

_____

_____

Thank you.

## PERSONS TO BE NOTIFIED

Name

Relationship

Address

Phone

Name

Relationship

Address

Phone

Name

Relationship

Address

Phone

Name

Relationship

Address

Phone

Name

Relationship

Address

Phone

Name

Relationship

Address

Phone

Name

Relationship

Address

Phone

Name

Relationship

Address

Phone

## KEY ADVISORS AND INSTITUTIONS
## TO BE CONTACTED

# My Funeral Arrangement Choices

## ANATOMICAL AND DISPOSITION INFORMATION

I ❑ do ❑ do not have an organ donor card.

Upon my death, I wish to donate the organs checked below:

❑ Heart ❑ Lungs ❑ Kidneys ❑ Liver

❑ Skin ❑ Bone ❑ Corneas

If not required, I ❑ will ❑ will not permit an autopsy.

I ❑ do ❑ do not wish for my body to be embalmed.

Upon my death, I wish for my body to be:

❑ cremated ❑ buried ❑ entombed or

❑ donated to medicine (preferred institution):

I ❑ have ❑ have not made arrangements for donating my body.

Donation arrangements have been made through

I have chosen _____

funeral establishment to handle my funeral.


I have ☐  have not ☐  premade my funeral arrangements.

I have ☐  have not ☐  prepaid my funeral expenses.


The contracts for the above prearrangements are located in

_____


I ☐ have ☐ have not purchased cemetery space with

_____


The contract for this purchase is located

_____

# CREMATION INSTRUCTIONS

I ☐ have ☐ have not purchased cremation services from

The contract for this purchase is located

Please remove all jewelry before cremation and return to

The type of cremation container I prefer is

Cremation remains ☐ should ☐ should not be present at the service.

☐ I would like my ashes

☐ buried ☐ entombed

☐ scattered at (location): _____

☐ I wish my cremated remains returned to (name)

## CEREMONY PREFERENCES

I ☐ do ☐ do not wish to have a visitation.

☐ public ☐ private visitation; casket ☐ open ☐ closed

Visitation location and time(s) _____

I would like:

☐ a traditional funeral, with a graveside service

☐ a traditional funeral, without a graveside service

☐ a graveside-only service

☐ a memorial service (without the body present)

☐ other: _____

_____

☐ no service

These are my preferences for:

Location of service _____

Clergy/officiate _____

Special music/hymns _____

_____

_____

Organist/soloist/other _____

People to speak

Scriptures/poems/other to be read

Flowers

Memorial donations made to

Photographs or possessions to be displayed

## MY CHOICE OF FUNERAL HOME SERVICES

I have selected _____

Funeral Home located at _____

_____

Phone _____ to provide the services I have

indicated below and ☐ have ☐ have not prepaid for those

services. My contract/receipt for prepaid services is located

_____

If I have not made arrangements already, I would like the

arrangements to include the following:

☐ arrangements conference with family or responsible party

☐ coordination with cemetery, crematory, or other parties
involved with disposition

☐ preparation and filing of necessary notices, permits,
authorizations

☐ temporary storage of the remains

☐ embalming

☐ dressing and hair care

☐ casket in the ☐ low ☐ medium ☐ high price range

☐ vault in the ☐ low ☐ medium ☐ high price range

☐ cremation container in the ☐ low ☐ medium
☐ high price range

Other thoughts about my funeral service:

# THINGS TO BE CANCELED

## Credit Cards

Type (VISA, MasterCard, Discover, American Express, Other)

———————————————————————————————————————————

Account # ————————————————————— Phone ——————————

Type (VISA, MasterCard, Discover, American Express, Other)

———————————————————————————————————————————

Account # ————————————————————— Phone ——————————

Type (VISA, MasterCard, Discover, American Express, Other)

———————————————————————————————————————————

Account # ————————————————————— Phone ——————————

Type (VISA, MasterCard, Discover, American Express, Other)

———————————————————————————————————————————

Account # ————————————————————— Phone ——————————

## Store Charge Cards

Store _____ Location _____

Account # _____ Phone _____


Store _____ Location _____

Account # _____ Phone _____


Store _____ Location _____

Account # _____ Phone _____


## Print and Electronic Subscriptions

Newspaper _____ Phone _____

Newsletter _____ Phone _____

Online service _____ Phone _____

Telephone _____ Phone _____

Cable TV _____ Phone _____

# Why You Need a Last Will and Testament

A Last Will and Testament can help you and your family in a number
of ways:

- It helps your family settle your financial affairs.
- It helps your family avoid disputes over how to distribute
  property after your death, especially items of sentimental value.
- It enables you to name a guardian for your minor children.
- It enables you to name someone you trust to act as your
  personal representative. This person will handle your financial
  affairs, such as debts.
- It enables you to take advantage of strategies to reduce federal
  estate taxes.

If you don't have a Last Will and Testament, your family will need to
deal with a number of problems upon your death:

- The state might determine the future of your minor children.
- State law determines how your assets and property are
  distributed.
- Your family has to deal with the pain of your loss and then
  with the court system in distributing your assets.
- You will not be able to take best advantage of strategies for
  reducing federal estate taxes.
- Heirs may argue over who gets what.

So be sure to write a Last Will and Testament, have it witnessed and
notarized, and put in a safe place where it can be accessed after your
death without legal intervention (i.e., not in your safe deposit box).

My Last Will and Testament is located _____

## SAMPLE LAST WILL AND TESTAMENT

# Last Will and Testament
# of

_____

I, _____ , of _____ ,

_____ , _____ , _____ (city, state, zip),

being of sound and disposing mind, do hereby make, publish, and

declare this my Last Will and Testament. I hereby revoke and annul

all wills, codicils, and other testamentary dispositions heretofore

made by me.

*First*, it is my will that all my just debts and funeral expenses shall be

paid from my estate by my executor, hereinafter named, as soon after

my decease as shall be convenient.

*Second*, I give, devise, and bequeath a tithe (one tenth) of my

remaining financial assets (exclusive of personal property and real

estate) to _____ (charitable or

religious organization) of _____,

_____,

_____, _____(address, city, state, zip) to do

with as they see fit.

*Third*, I give, devise, and bequeath _____

_____

_____ (items and/or amounts) to

_____,

_____,

_____, _____(address, city, state, zip) to do

with as he/she/they see fit.

All the rest and residue of my estate, both real, personal and mixed, I

give, devise and bequeath to _____

_____,

_____, _____(address, city, state, zip) and

to his/her heirs and assigns forever.

Inasmuch as my estate is making a contribution to charity prior to further distributions, it is my wish that the remaining heirs feel no obligation to donate a further tithe of this inheritance.

*And last*, I do hereby nominate, constitute and appoint _____

_____, of

_____,

_____, _____ (address, city, state, zip)

executor of this, my Last Will and Testament, and I desire that s/he shall not be required to give bond for the faithful performance of the duties of that office.

*In testimony Whereof*, I had set my hand and seal to this, my Last Will and Testament, at _____ County,

_____, _____,

(city, state) this _____ day of _____ (month), in the year of our Lord, _____ .

_____

_____ [SEAL]

*Signed, Sealed, Published and Declared,* by _____ ,

the above-named testator, as and for his/her Last Will and

Testament, in our presence, and at his/her request, and in his/her

presence, and in the presence of each other, we have hereunto

subscribed our names as attesting witnesses.

_____        _____

of _____     of _____

_____        _____

WITNESS my hand and Notarial Seal the day and year

aforesaid

_____

Notary Public, State of _____

_____

Print Name

_____

My Commission Expires

# Asset Information

## LIFE INSURANCE POLICIES

Policy number and company _____

Type* _____ Insured _____

Owner** _____

Primary beneficiary _____

Secondary _____

Who pays premium** _____

Cash value _____

Amount of loans on policy _____

Face amount _____


Policy number and company _____

Type* _____ Insured _____

Owner** _____

Primary beneficiary _____

Secondary _____

---

*Term, whole life, split dollar, group life, annuity.
**Husband (H), wife (W), corporation (C).

Who pays premium** _____

Cash value _____

Amount of loans on policy _____

Face amount _____


Policy number and company _____

Type* _____ Insured _____

Owner** _____

Primary beneficiary _____

Secondary _____

Who pays premium** _____

Cash value _____

Amount of loans on policy _____

Face amount _____

---

*Term, whole life, split dollar, group life, annuity.
**Husband (H), wife (W), corporation (C).

# BANK ACCOUNT(S)
# AND SAFE DEPOSIT BOX(ES)

### Account #1

Name on Account: _____

Account Number: _____

Account Type: _____

Branch Name and Address: _____

_____

### Account #2

Name on Account: _____

Account Number: _____

Account Type: _____

Branch Name and Address: _____

_____

**Account #3**

Name on Account: _____

Account Number: _____

Account Type: _____

Branch Name and Address: _____

_____

**Safe Deposit Box**

Safety Deposit Box Located at: _____

_____

Location of Key(s): _____

_____

# BROKERAGE ACCOUNTS

Name of broker _____

Account # _____ Phone _____

Name of broker _____

Account # _____ Phone _____

Name of broker _____

Account # _____ Phone _____

Name of broker _____

Account # _____ Phone _____

Name of broker _____

Account # _____ Phone _____

Name of broker _____

Account # _____ Phone _____

Name of broker _____

Account # _____ Phone _____

## STOCKS AND BONDS HELD AT HOME
## OR IN SAFE DEPOSIT BOX(ES)

Company _____ # of Shares _____

Company _____ # of Shares _____

Company _____ # of Shares _____

Company _____ # of Shares _____

Company _____ # of Shares _____

Company _____ # of Shares _____

Company _____ # of Shares _____

Company _____ # of Shares _____

Company _____ # of Shares _____

Company _____ # of Shares _____

Company _____ # of Shares _____

Company _____ # of Shares _____

Company _____ # of Shares _____

Company _____ # of Shares _____

Company _____ # of Shares _____

## OTHER INVESTMENTS

Mutual Fund _____

Account # _____ Phone _____

Mutual Fund _____

Account # _____ Phone _____

Mutual Fund _____

Account # _____ Phone _____

Mutual Fund _____

Account # _____ Phone _____

Oil or Gas Well company _____

Location _____ Phone _____

Oil or Gas Well company _____

Location _____ Phone _____

Precious Metals type _____

Where held _____ Amount _____

Precious Metals type _____

Where held _____ Amount _____

## TANGIBLE PERSONAL PROPERTY INVENTORY

It is advisable to have an inventory of your personal property for a number of reasons. For example, if you have a loss due to fire or theft, a property inventory will help you greatly in recovering money from your insurance company. It will also help you when you fill out the form designating your wishes for disbursement of some of these items.

You may write your list below, or even use computer software to track your personal property. If you choose not to write it here, the location where you keep it is

_____

**Inventory**

_____

_____

_____

_____

_____

_____

_____

_____

# DISBURSEMENT OF SPECIAL ITEMS

As you walk around your home and look back on your life, there may
be items and belongings that you treasure, that hold a significant
value for you. Most of these may come with sentiments and
memories that render them priceless. Start now to list these and then
to name the persons whom you would like to receive them when you
die.

| ITEM DESCRIPTION | BEQUEATHED TO |
|---|---|
| | |
| | |
| | |
| | |
| | |
| | |
| | |
| | |
| | |
| | |
| | |

# LIVING TRUSTS

There are some special situations where it is advantageous to have one or more living trusts, either in addition to or instead of a Last Will and Testament. Each of those is unique to the individual, and should be prepared by a lawyer and/or a certified estate planner.

If you have a living trust, this is the place to say so, and indicate where it can be found.

I ☐ do   ☐ do not have a living trust.

It is located _____ .

# Things I May Not Have Told You Yet

## STATEMENT OF WISHES

To My Family:

We have become used to consulting each other when making decisions throughout our lifetime. When I am physically gone from you, if you are unsure about what my wishes might be in certain matters of concern, I have noted some thoughts below that might help to guide you in this process.

_____

_____

_____

_____

_____

_____

_____

_____

_____

_____

_____

_____

## SPECIAL MESSAGES TO THOSE I LOVE

# Last Minute Changes

## SPECIAL INSTRUCTIONS AND INFORMATION

Use this page to keep current updates on pertinent information:

_____

_____

_____

_____

_____

_____

_____

_____

_____

_____

_____

_____

_____

_____

# acknowledgements

Many people have encouraged this effort and have walked with me each step of the way. Their prayers and mentoring have proved invaluable. When I was lost, they gently showed me the way, shared their stories with me, and taught me again and again the value of listening. Many served as connectors leading me to new sources and resources. All have revealed themselves to me with remarkable honesty. I have been humbled and privileged and eternally grateful. I can only list some of their names and trust that all will know that their spirits flow through this entire book.

They are the community of Kittamaqundi and the Reverend Jerry Goethe, Morris Keeton, Florence and Rick Miller, Judy Colligan, Buthaina and Mike Potash, Charles and Edith Seashore, Anne Marie Zwycewicz, Tom Bishop, Claudia Norris, Marie Moore, Gerry Landrum, Janis Cripe, Linda Goldman, Ellen Zinner, Charles Cockey, Jack Dunlavey, Sam Nissen, Frank Turban, Sue Cavendish, Beverly Roberts, Elaine Benson, George Pappas, Carole and Harvey Ratner, Marsha Broaddus, Patricia Fisher, Joyce Lindenmuth, John Reusing, Kibibi Mack-Shelton, Brian Whitmer, The Reverends Corinne and Wesley Baker, Diana Bamford-Rees, Eileen Borland, Kathleen and Bob Engelbach; Anne Nissen, who, on our daily walks, suffered with me over every chapter; Randy Malm for his gift of creating forms; Bob Anderman, Frederic Johnston, and Normale Doyle, who rescued me time and again from computer attacks; and our enduring spirits who live forever in and with us.

To my husband Dennis Cochran; my children, Teresa, Robyn and Billy; my sons-in-law Fred and Rick, my sister Gerri, and brother-in-law Steve; and brothers, Ashley and Butch, for their unfailing belief in me, I thank you. To my niece and nephew, Jessica and Robby, who understand and accept that we must die, thank you for your wisdom. To the staff of Pioneer Custom Cleaning and especially Audré Aaron, who cheered me on, thank you. To Mom, who promises that I no longer will have to throw her in the street, and a special thank you to my family for sharing "Dad's Story." While I was completing this manuscript, we were brought together suddenly by the death of our father.

I am especially touched by all those who contributed their stories and who agreed, every one, to use of their real names, the common thread to their response being: If it will help someone, it will be my privilege. Thank you all.

To my publisher, Kathleen Hughes at Capital Books, who has been a gracious, sensitive, and generous presence throughout all of our communications. God blessed me when I was led to you. Thank you for your understanding and support.

Special acknowledgement to Wesley Baker (my religion consultant), Ira Byock, Shep Jeffries, Gerald May, and Ellen Zinner for their generous reviews.

I am especially grateful to Julia Mayo, who in her lifetime touched me in a special way and caused me to open up to that "still small voice." You will forever live in me.

# Contributors

Francis Leonard, Jr.—Frankie's Story
Dennis Cochran—Dennis's Story
Patricia Husted—Patsy's Story
Frederic N. Johnston—Fred's Story
Linda Barczak—Linda's Story
Anne Nissen—Anne's Story
George Hancock—George's Story
Marilyn Anderman— Marilyn's Story
Kenneth Cotich—Ken's Story
Ann Norris—Alice's Story
Morris Keeton—Morris's Story and More of Morris's Story
Jack Dunlavey—Jack's Story
Corinne Baker—A Father's Day Message
Jack Daniel—J. Mitchell's Story
Rhona Schonwald—Rhona's Story
Lutfi On—Lutfi's Story
Khaled and Samar Eloseily—Khaled and Samar's Story

Ellen Zinner— Ellen's Story
Carole Ratner—Carole's Story
William Hug—Bill's Story, Grieving is Living
Jo Samels—Jo's Story
Carol Newman—Prologue and Epilogue
John F. Keener—Sibling Education
Phil Sosis—Connections

# suggested readings

Bernard, Jan Selliken, and Miriam Schneider. *The True Work of Dying: A Practical and Compassionate Guide to Easing the Dying Process*. New York: Avon Books, 1996.

Byock, I. *Dying Well: The Prospect for Growth at the End of Life*. New York: Riverhead/Putnam, 1997. www.dyingwell.org

Callahan, Maggie, and Patricia Kelley. *Final Gifts Understanding the Special Awareness, Needs, and Communications of the Dying*. New York: Poseidon Press, 1992.

De Hennezel, Marie. *Intimate Death: How the Dying Teach Us How to Live*. Translated by Carol Brown Janeway. New York: Alfred A. Knopf, 1997.

Dunn, Hank. *Hard Choices for Loving People: CPR, Artificial Feeding, Comfort Measures, and the Elderly Patient*. Virginia: A & A Publishers, 1993.

Goldman, Linda. *Breaking the Silence: A Guide to Help Children with Complicated Grief—Suicide, Homicide, Aids, Violence, and Abuse*. Washington: Accelerated Development, 1996.

Hill, T. Patrick, and David Shirley. *A Good Death: Taking More Control at the End of Your Life*. Choice in Dying, Inc., The National Council for the Right to Die. New York: Addison-Wesley Publishing Company, 1992.

Kramer, Kenneth. *The Sacred Art of Dying: How World Religions Understand Death*. New York: Paulist Press, 1988.

Levine, Stephen. *Who Dies?: An Investigation into Conscious Living and Conscious Dying*. New York: Doubleday, 1982.

———. *A Gradual Awakening.* New York: Anchor Books/Doubleday, 1989.

Lord, Janice Harris. *No Time for Goodbyes: Coping with Sorrow, Anger and Injustice After a Tragic Death, fourth ed.* Ventura, CA: Pathfinder Publishing, 1991.

Lynn, Joanne. *Handbook for Mortals: Guidance for People Facing Serious Illness.* New York: Oxford University Press, 1999.

McNees, Pat. *Dying: A Book of Comfort.* New York: Warner Books, 1996.

Morse, Melvin, M.D., with Paul Perry. *Closer to the Light: Learning from the Near-Death Experiences of Children.* New York: Ivy Books, 1990.

Tatelbaum, Judy. *The Courage to Grieve.* New York: Harper & Row, 1982.

# resources

National Hospice and Palliative Care Organization
1700 Diagonal Road, Suite 300
Alexandria, VA 22314
703-243-5900
*www.nhpco.org*

Hospice Foundation of America
2001 S Street, NW #300
Washington, DC 20009
1-800-854-3402
*www.hospicefoundation.org*

Children's Hospice International
2202 Mt. Vernon Avenue, Suite 3C
Alexandria, VA 22301
703-684-0330
*www.chionline.org*

Partnership for Caring, Inc. a Choice in Dying
1035 30th Street, NW
Washington, DC 20007
1-800-989-9455
*www.partnershipforcaring.org*
(24-hour hotline offering counseling, pain management information and downloadable state-specific advance directives)

Aging With Dignity
P.O. Box 1661
Tallahassee, FL 32302
*www.agingwithdignity.org*
(offers "Five Wishes," an easy to understand 8-page form that guides people in completing advance directives. Available in English and Spanish.)

AARP
601 E Street, NW
Washington, DC 20049
1-800-424-3410
*www.aarp.org/programs*

Association for Death Education and Counseling (ADEC)
324 North Main Street
West Hartford, CT 06117-2507
860-586-7503
*www.adec.org*

The Grief Recovery Institute
P.O. Box 461659
Los Angeles, CA 90046-1659
*www.grief-recovery.com*

Compassionate Friends, Inc.
(helping parents who have lost a child)
*www.compassionatefriends.org*

National Runaway Switchboard
(*local* suicide hotline will be referred to callers)
1-800-621-4000
*www.nrscrisisline.org*

National STD and AIDS Hotline
1-800-342-AIDS
*www.cdcnpin.org*

The Department of Veterans Affairs
1-800-827-1000
*www.va.gov*

Social Security Administration
1-800-722-1213
*www.ssa.gov*

Medicare
1-800-633-4227
*www.medicare.gov*

Association of Personal Historians (AHP)
*www.personalhistorians.org*

# index

# about the author

Pat Cochran lives in Columbia, Maryland with her husband Dennis and together they have six grown children. She is active in her faith community, tennis, local theater, and is most actively involved in her family, now expanded with spouses, grandchildren, and a newly arrived granddaughter. She loves art, music, dancing, gardening, decorating, and her zany and unpredictable husband.

# last rights workshop

We are happy to offer a day-long workshop, based on this book, that provides a safe and comfortable place to discuss and plan for your own death. This day is yours to gather information and create a personal map for your end-of-life journey. During this day you will share your stories, write your eulogies and living wills and consider body disposition options. Doing all of these with intention helps us to move through mental blocks regarding death, and opens up a space for life celebrations, values clarification, and healing attitudes. Dramatic presentations, small and large group discussions, guided meditations, and humor give this workshop an added dimension. We hope this day will create for you a merging of body, mind, and spirit in the experience of living and dying.

This workshop is for family, friends, and business associates. We especially encourage healthcare professionals, clergy, and members of the legal community to attend. Your congregation, club, or organization may also be interested in sponsoring this workshop. Contact us at:

Last Rights
5430 Lynx Lane, #348
Columbia, MD 21044
301-854-1475

Visit us at:
*www.lastrightsweb.com*

Or e-mail Pat at:
*patcochran@home.com*

We are happy to answer any questions about our workshops and presentations, and to provide you with our current schedule.